DENVER LANDMARKS

by Langdon E. Morris, Jr., aia

photos: Melvyn E. Schieltz

Charles W. Cleworth, Publisher Denver, Colorado

Photography: Melvyn E. Schieltz
Graphic Design: Graphic Impressions, Inc.
Editorial Assistance: Candace Bradford,
Jane Merriken
Cartography: J. A. Sundquist
Typography: David Rile
Research Assistance:
David A. Wicks, Denver Planning Office
The Denver Public Library, Western History Department

Library of Congress Catalog Number: 79-51647
International Standard Book Number: 0-934212-00-7
Printed in the United States of America

Contents

Introduction

This book was undertaken because Charles W. ("Cal") Cleworth recognized the need for a guide to the historic landmarks of Denver. With this in mind he proposed that we collaborate on its production—I as writer, he as publisher—to which I readily agreed since I have long been frustrated by the lack of such a guide.

While Cal is unmistakably a publisher, I am unmistakably not a writer—nor a scholar, for that matter. This book, then, is essentially a collection of superb photographs of landmark buildings by Mel Schieltz, each accompanied by brief descriptive data compiled from the files of the Denver Landmark Preservation Commission.

Since its inception in April 1967, the Landmark Commission has nominated eight districts and 113 individual structures that were built, predominantly, in the late nineteenth century. As might be anticipated, more than half of the designated landmarks are houses, although contrary to popular opinion only three are classified as "mansions." Of the balance, twenty-three designations are churches. And of the scores of outstanding commercial structures that once graced downtown Denver, only seventeen are landmarks—a sad commentary on the American preoccupation with "progress." It is interesting to note that the work (almost all houses) of architect Frederick J. Sterner is represented eleven times, while that of Denver's greatest and most prolific commercial architect, Frank E. Edbrooke, appears only three times.

The book is arranged by general areas of landmark concentration, each introduced with a map locating the individual landmark by a number correlated with the photographs and descriptions that follow. Outlying, scattered landmarks are located on an overall map of Denver, upon which are also indicated the locations of the general areas of concentration.

Although its members encouraged me to write this book, it is not an official publication of the Landmark Commission, and the opinions expressed herein are solely my own. Much historical data is missing, and perhaps some included is inaccurate; but it was beyond the scope of this effort to engage in any original research or more thorough documentation. For any errors that may occur, I offer my sincere apologies.

Langdon E. Morris, Jr., AIA *May 1979*

This book is dedicated to those members of the Denver City Council who have held office since the inception of the Denver Landmark Preservation Commission in April 1967.

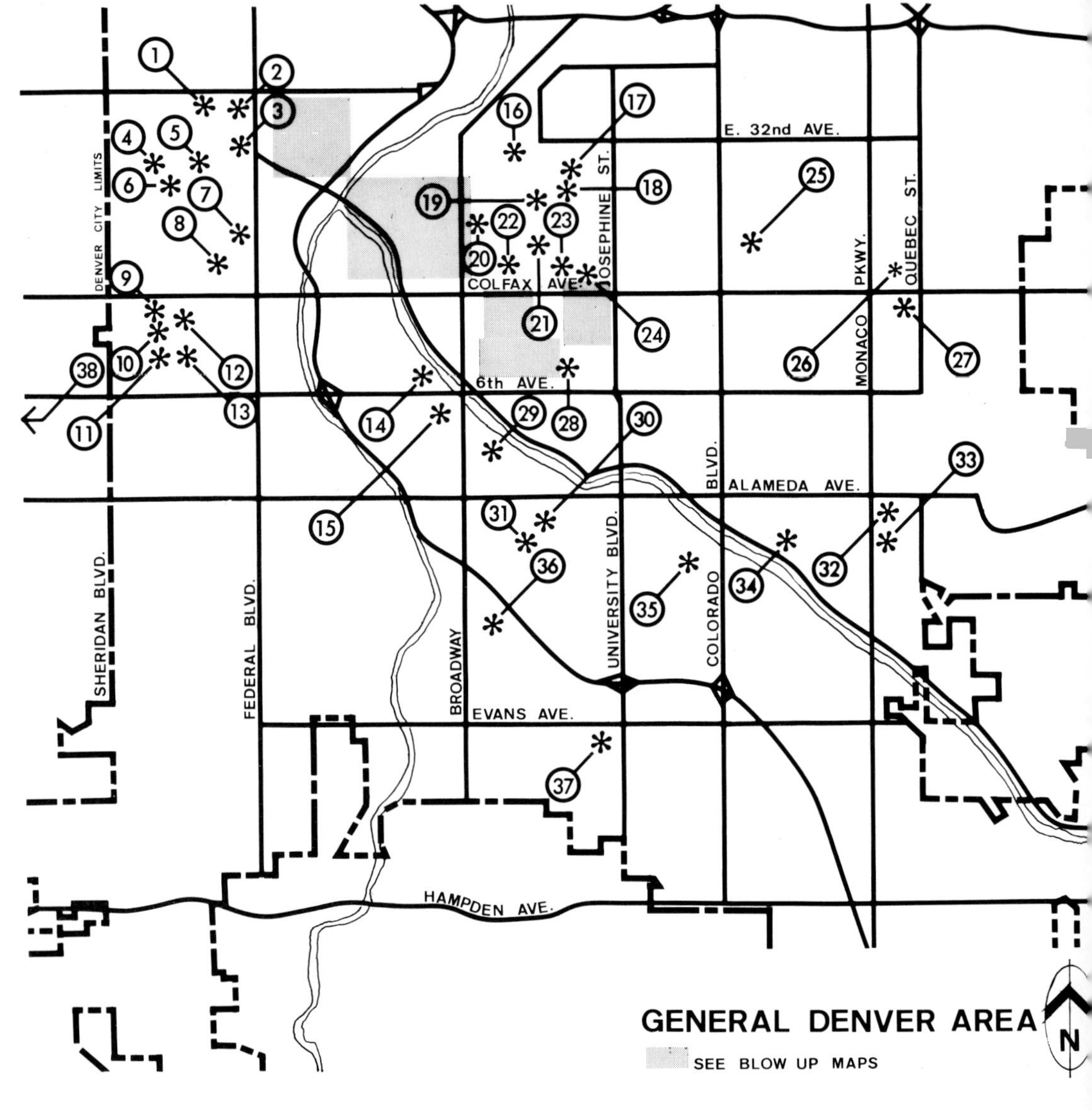

GENERAL DENVER AREA
SEE BLOW UP MAPS
N
E. 32nd AVE.
COLFAX AVE.
6th AVE.
ALAMEDA AVE.
EVANS AVE.
HAMPDEN AVE.
DENVER CITY LIMITS
SHERIDAN BLVD.
FEDERAL BLVD.
BROADWAY
UNIVERSITY BLVD.
COLORADO BLVD.
JOSEPHINE ST.
MONACO PKWY.
QUEBEC ST.
1
2
3
4
5
6
7
8
9
10
11
12
13
14
15
16
17
18
19
20
21
22
23
24
25
26
27
28
29
30
31
32
33
34
35
36
37
38

A. General Denver Area

1. The John Brisben Walker House
3520 Newton Street

This house, built by master stonemason David Cox, Sr., was commissioned by John Brisben Walker (but lived in by his brother Bolivar). John Brisben, a man of many talents, during his lifetime owned, edited, and published Cosmopolitan *magazine, helped establish the Denver Mountain Parks system, developed Red Rocks Park, and built a cog railroad up Mount Morrison.*

Construction Date: *1885*
Architect: *David Cox, Sr.*
Style: *Builder vernacular*
Designation Number 44; November 26, 1973

2. The Cox (Gargoyle) House
3425 Lowell Boulevard

Built by David Cox, Sr., for his own use, this house is distinguished for its outstanding craftsmanship, if not for its design. The elaborate stone carving at the main gable and the gargoyles at the porch roof corners are particularly notable.

Construction Date: *1892*
Architect: *David Cox, Sr.*
Style: *Victorian*
Designation Number 42; November 26, 1973
(listed on National Register)

3. The Cox House

3417 Lowell Boulevard

Master stonemason David Cox, Sr., built this house for one of his many daughters. It is notable for the size of the dressed sandstone slabs used on its exterior walls.

(See also: 3425 Lowell Boulevard.)

Construction Date: *1908*
Architect: *David Cox, Sr.*
Style: *Not definable*
Designation Number 41; November 26, 1973

4. **Residence**
2851 Perry Street

This house was built by the Veddar family and has been occupied since 1915 by the Lobach family, of whom the present owner, Grace Lobach Woodbury, is a descendant. Mrs. Woodbury is the widow of Frank S. Woodbury, a prominent Denver publisher, banker, and philanthropist.

Construction Date: *1893*
Architect: *Not known*
Style: *Queen Anne*
Designation Number 112; January 21, 1979

2847
SPEED
LIMIT
25

5. Residence
2841 Perry Street

Also built by the Veddar family and also owned at one time by Mrs. Grace L. Woodbury, it is a companion house to 2851 Perry Street. The floor plans and massing of the two are identical, differing only in the intricately carved details of the exterior.

Construction Date: *1894*
Architect: *Not known*
Style: *Queen Anne*
Designation Number 113; January 21, 1979

3016

6. The Hermann H. Heiser House

3016 Osceola Street

This house was built for Hermann H. Heiser, who established a successful saddlery business in Denver after migrating from Saxony in 1854. Both his company and his family were prominent in early Denver history. The house is a good example of the Queen Anne style, with its corner tower, open porches, and small-scale classical details. The original iron cresting at the rooftop has been removed.

Construction Date: *1892*
Architect: *Not known*
Style: *Late Queen Anne*
Designation Number 38; November 26, 1973

7. Residence
2143 Grove Street

This elaborately detailed house was built for Frederick Neef, owner and operator of the well-known Neef Brothers Brewery. Combining both Eastlake and Queen Anne architectural features, it ably demonstrates the Victorian preoccupation with complicated volumes and elaborate ornamentation.

Construction Date: *1886*
Architect: *Not known (probably from a pattern book)*
Style: *Queen Anne/Eastlake*
Designation Number 83; September 28, 1975

8. Residence
3205 West Twenty-first Avenue

This house is a wonderful example of Victorian "pattern book" design. Carefully restored in recent years, it was probably constructed in the early 1890s (a surmise based on the surviving details, assuming they are original).

Construction Date: *Circa 1892*
Architect: *Not known*
Style: *Victorian*
Designation Number 71; November 19, 1974

9. The Ralph Voorhees House

1471 Stuart Street

This house, which Ralph Voorhees built for himself, was one of seven he constructed in the immediate area as developer of the West Colfax Subdivision. Five of the seven houses are Denver landmarks known as the Stuart Street Group. Voorhees was a developer, a member of the Colorado legislature (where he "fathered" Colorado's Flag Day), and a founder of Colorado Women's College.

Construction Date: *1890*
Architect: *Lang and Pugh*
Style: *Richardsonian Romanesque*
Designation Number 68; November 16, 1974

10. Residence

1435 Stuart Street

The second Voorhees house to receive landmark designation is considerably more interesting architecturally than the first. Especially noteworthy is the unusual window on the south facade.

Construction Date: *1890*
Architect: *Lang and Pugh*
Style: *Richardsonian Romanesque*
Designation Number 69; November 16, 1974

11. Residence
1389 Stuart Street

A totally different architectural style distinguishes the third Voorhees house from the first two, although it was designed by the same architects. The ground floor masonry has been stuccoed over, detracting a great deal from its appearance.

Construction Date: *1892*
Architect: *Lang and Pugh*
Style: *Shingle*
Designation Number 72; January 27, 1975

12. Residence
1444 Stuart Street

Fortunately, the fourth of the Stuart Street designations has not been stuccoed over, so it remains a relatively pure example of the style—although the inept porch remodeling comes close to destroying the visual significance of the house.

Construction Date: *1888*
Architect: *William Lang*
Style: *Shingle*
Designation Number 89; March 21, 1976

13. Residence
1390 Stuart Street

The last of the houses in the Stuart Street Group to be designated (because of owner objections), this is one of the most charming and stylistically obvious. Extensively restored within the last year, it is now used for offices.

Construction Date: *1891*
Architect: *Lang and Pugh*
Style: *Queen Anne*
Designation Number 111; January 7, 1979

BUCKHORN EXCHANGE

14. The Buckhorn Exchange Restaurant Building

1000 Osage Street

This building rose to prominence in 1893, when it became the Rio Grande Exchange Restaurant and Saloon, operated by Henry H. Zietz. Later under the management of Harry H. Zietz, Jr., its name was changed to Buckhorn Exchange Restaurant. Notable for its display of photographs, firearms, artifacts, hunting trophies, and its 1857 German-built bar, it has been recently restored and reopened by new owners.

Construction Date: *1885*
Architect: *Not known*
Style: *Victorian Commercial*
Designation Number 27; August 28, 1972

532

15. The Coyle-Chase House
532 West Fourth Avenue

This charming small house was indeed the early home of Mary Coyle Chase, internationally known author of Bernadine, Mrs. McThing, *and that most popular American play* Harvey.

Construction Date: *1891*
Architect: *Not known*
Style: *Victorian (builder vernacular)*
Designation Number 78; May 18, 1975

16. Sacred Heart Church
2760 Larimer Street

This church was the first permanent home of the Jesuit Order in Denver and also the third Catholic parish established in Denver. It was for a period of time the worship place of H.A.W. and Baby Doe Tabor.

Construction Date: *1889*
Architect: *Scott Anthony*
Style: *High Victorian Gothic*
Designation Number 35; September 24, 1973

17: Residence
2501 High Street

Built of rusticated Castle Rock lava stone and sandstone, it is similar in detailing to the house of master stonemason David Cox, Sr., and is attributed to him. His structures are generally considered to represent the best of nineteenth century craftsmanship.

Construction Date: *1902*
Architect: *Attributed to David Cox, Sr.*
Style: *Not definable*
Designation Number 43; November 26, 1973

18. The Walters House
2259 Gilpin Street

Constructed for John Walters, a prominent sheepman and founder of the Standard Meat Company, it continued as a residence for the Walters family until 1944.

Construction Date: *1888*
Architect: *Not known*
Style: *Victorian*
Designation Number 107; April 23, 1978

19. Zion Baptist Church

933 East Twenty-fourth Avenue

Constructed as the Calvary Baptist Church in 1892, it was sold to the Zion Baptist Church in 1911. This congregation, established in 1865 at Twentieth and Arapahoe streets by former slaves, is considered the oldest predominantly black Baptist church in Colorado.

Construction Date: *1892*
Architect: *Not known*
Style: *Richardsonian Romanesque*
Designation Number 13; April 19, 1969

20. The Thomas Hornsby Ferril House

2123 Downing Street

Built by Mrs. John Palmer, Thomas Hornsby Ferril's great-aunt, it has been occupied continuously by the Ferril family since its completion. Ferril's father, Will C. Ferril, was city editor of several Denver newspapers and editor and publisher of the Rocky Mountain Herald. *Thomas Hornsby Ferril, who succeeded his father as editor and publisher of the* Rocky Mountain Herald, *is one of America's great poets and an important figure in the literary and cultural history of Colorado.*

Construction Date: *1889*
Architect: *Not known*
Style: *Victorian Eclectic*
Designation Number 36; September 24, 1973

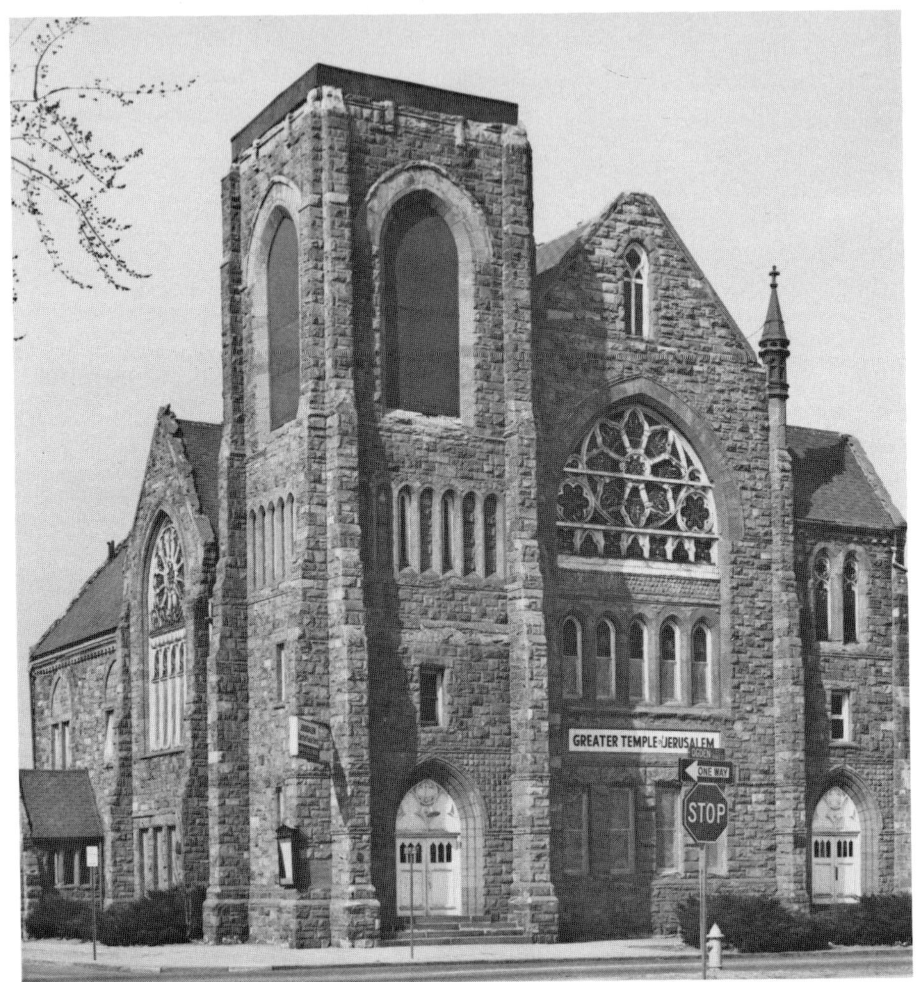
GREATER TEMPLE OF JERUSALEM
ONE WAY
STOP

21. Scott Methodist Church
2201 Ogden Street

Constructed as the Christ Methodist Episcopal Church, it was renamed in 1927 to honor Bishop I. B. Scott, the first black to do Methodist missionary work in Africa.

The steeple had to be removed in 1976 because of wind damage.

Construction Date: *1889*
Architect: *Franklin Kidder*
Style: *High Victorian Gothic*
Designation Number 18; February 14, 1970

22. The Frank E. Edbrooke House

931 East Seventeenth Avenue

Denver's greatest nineteenth century architect, Frank E. Edbrooke, designed this house for himself in 1893. During a remarkable Denver career spanning the thirty-five years between 1880 and 1915, Edbrooke designed a wide range of buildings, including the Masonic Temple, the Brown Palace Hotel, the Central Presbyterian Church, the Denver Dry Goods Company Building, and the Hotel Metropole (now the south half of the Cosmopolitan Hotel). Perhaps his finest building was the People's National Savings Bank (1889), unfortunately and unnecessarily demolished in DURA's great sweep, the Skyline urban renewal project.

Construction Date: *1893*
Architect: *Frank E. Edbrooke*
Style: *Queen Anne*
Designation Number 110; January 7, 1979

23. Pearce-McAllister Cottage
1880 Gaylord Street

Constructed for Harold Pearce, who was then general manager of the famous Argo Smelter, it was subsequently sold to Henry McAllister, general counsel for the Denver and Rio Grande Railroad. The cottage is now owned by the state and has been in use by the State Historical Society. Designed by a master architect, it is an interesting combination of architectural styles, displaying a gambrel roof, Georgian details, and Victorian dormers.

Construction Date: *1899*
Architect: *Frederick J. Sterner*
Style: *Victorian Eclectic*
Designation Number 25; August 28, 1972
(listed on National Register)

24. The Smith House

1801 York Street

This house was constructed for his son, Frank L. Smith, by Eben Smith, who established Colorado's first stamp mill (with Jerome B. Chafee), was an organizer of the First National Bank of Denver, and built a railroad between Florence and Cripple Creek.

Construction Date: *1905*
Architect: *Fisher and Huntington*
Style: *Predominantly Neoclassical Revival*
Designation Number 22; November 27, 1971

25. St. Thomas Episcopal Church

2201 Dexter Street

This building is probably the finest Denver example of the lavish Spanish baroque style so often seen in Mexico. The elaborately carved stone entrance way is especially noteworthy.

Construction Date: *1908*
Architect: *Harry C. Manning*
Style: *Spanish Colonial Revival*
Designation Number 97; April 24, 1977

26. Treat Hall

Montview Boulevard and Quebec Street

The first building on the Colorado Women's College campus, it housed the entire college for a number of years. Named in honor of the college's first president, Jay Porter Treat, its exterior reflects the diversity of functions contained within. The main entrance way is particularly notable.

Construction Date: *1889*
Architect: *Jackson and Betts*
Style: *Richardsonian Romanesque*
Designation Number 81; September 7, 1975 (listed on National Register)

27. St. Luke's Episcopal Church

1270 Poplar Street

Constructed both as a church for Montclair residents and as a chapel for the nearby Episcopal boys' school, Jarvis Hall, it has 1938 and 1953 additions to the south, which house the parish hall and educational facilities.

Construction Date: *1890*
Architect: *James Murdoch*
Style: *Early Gothic Revival*
Designation Number 82; September 28, 1975

28. The Kerr House

1900 East Seventh Avenue

Constructed for John G. Kerr, who operated a stone and marble quarry, it is notable for its use of carved Colorado travertine trim (from Kerr's own quarries, of course).

Construction Date: *1925*
Architect: *J. J. B. Benedict*
Style: *Benedict*
Designation Number 94; August 22, 1976

29. South Broadway Christian Church
23 Lincoln Street

Long a prominent neighborhood landmark, this church displays unusual visual excitement. Its picturesque medieval quality, enhanced by fine craftsmanship and rich carvings, defies precise stylistic definition.

Construction Date: *1891*
Architect: *Miller and Janisch*
Style: *Modified Romanesque*
Designation Number 15; April 19, 1969

30. The Eugene Field House
Washington Park

Constructed in the 1870s, this house is named for its one-time occupant, writer-critic-poet Eugene Field, who was managing editor of the Denver Tribune *from 1881 through 1883. When threatened with demolition, the building was purchased by the city and ultimately relocated through the efforts of Mrs. James Joseph ("Unsinkable Molly") Brown, thereby becoming Denver's first preservation endeavor.*

Construction Date: *1870s*
Architect: *Not known*
Style: *Builder vernacular*
Designation Number 48; November 26, 1973
(listed on National Register)

31. Smith's Ditch Historic District
Washington Park

Surveyed and constructed between 1860 and 1867, it was first called the "City Ditch" but became known as "Smith's Ditch" in 1865, when it was taken over and completed for its twenty-seven-mile length by John W. Smith. In 1875 it was purchased by the city of Denver and thereafter was commonly known as the "City Ditch." Only that portion of the ditch that extends through Washington Park has historic district designation.

Designation Number: District 7; April 24, 1977
(listed on National Register)

32. The Gate Lodge, Fairmont Cemetery
East Alameda Avenue and South Quebec Street

Obviously inspired by H. H. Richardson's F. L. Ames Gate Lodge in North Easton, Massachusetts, it nonetheless adheres closely to Richardson's popular "library style" in its massing and elements. This doubly Richardsonian building is not Romanesque, ironically, but Gothic (undoubtedly to maintain a consistent architectural relationship with the nearby Ivy Chapel).

Construction Date: *1890*
Architect: *Harry T. E. Wendell*
Style: *Early Gothic Revival*
Designation Number 87; February 8, 1976

33. The Ivy Chapel, Fairmont Cemetery

East Alameda Avenue and South Quebec Street

This charming little chapel, with its picturesque flying buttresses, is a fine Victorian example of the thirteenth century French Gothic style. Beautifully proportioned and consistently detailed, along with the nearby Gate Lodge, it definitely merits a visit.

Construction Date: *1890*
Architect: *Harry T. E. Wendell*
Style: *Late Gothic Revival*
Designation Number 88; February 8, 1976

34. Four Mile House

715 South Forest Street

Considered the oldest standing structure in Denver, it is located on the historic routes of the Smoky Hill Trail and the Old Cherokee Trail/Denver-Santa Fe Stage Road. The original portion of the house was constructed in 1859 by the Brantner Brothers. It was later purchased by Mary Cawker and was an early stopping place for trappers, Indians, emigrants, stagecoaches and wagons. Owned by the City and County of Denver, it is now undergoing a complete restoration.

Construction Date: *1858*
Architect: *Not known*
Style: *Victorian mixture*
Designation Number 12; December 21, 1968
(listed on National Register)

35. The Phipps Mansion (Belcaro)
3400 Belcaro Drive

Constructed for U.S. Senator and Mrs. Lawrence C. Phipps, it now serves as a conference center for the University of Denver. Of great size, situated on beautifully landscaped grounds, its exterior is sheathed in unusual hand-pressed, sand molded bricks.

Construction Date: *1932*
Architect: *Fisher and Fisher (William E. and Arthur A.) and Charles Platt (New York)*
Style: *Late Georgian Revival*
Designation Number 98; May 22, 1977
(listed on National Register)

PLATT

36. The James A. Fleming House

1500 South Grant Street

This stone house was constructed for the mayor of the city of South Denver in 1882 and subsequently served as South Denver's city hall, jail, and library. Since South Denver's annexation to Denver in 1894, the building has been used as a youth center and, currently, as a senior citizen activity center. It is distinguished by its matching two-story towers.

Construction Date: *1882*
Architect: *Not known*
Style: *Queen Anne*
Designation Number 51; November 26, 1973

37. Evans Memorial Chapel

University of Denver Campus

Originally located at Thirteenth and Bannock streets, this chapel was dismantled stone by stone in 1959 and reconstructed at its present site. The oldest Protestant church building still in use in Denver, it was built by John Evans as a memorial to his daughter, Josephine Evans Elbert.

Construction Date: *1878*
Architect: *Not known*
Style: *Early Gothic Revival*
Designation Number 16; April 19, 1969
(listed on National Register)

38. **Red Rocks Theater**
Morrison, Colorado

This magnificent, acoustically perfect open-air theater was actually begun in 1904 when John Brisben Walker purchased the land for resort development. Ultimately the city of Denver purchased the site (hence its designation although outside the city limits) and completed the theater as we know it today.

Construction Date: *1938*
Architect: *Burnham Hoyt*
Style: *Modern*
Designation Number 49; November 26, 1973

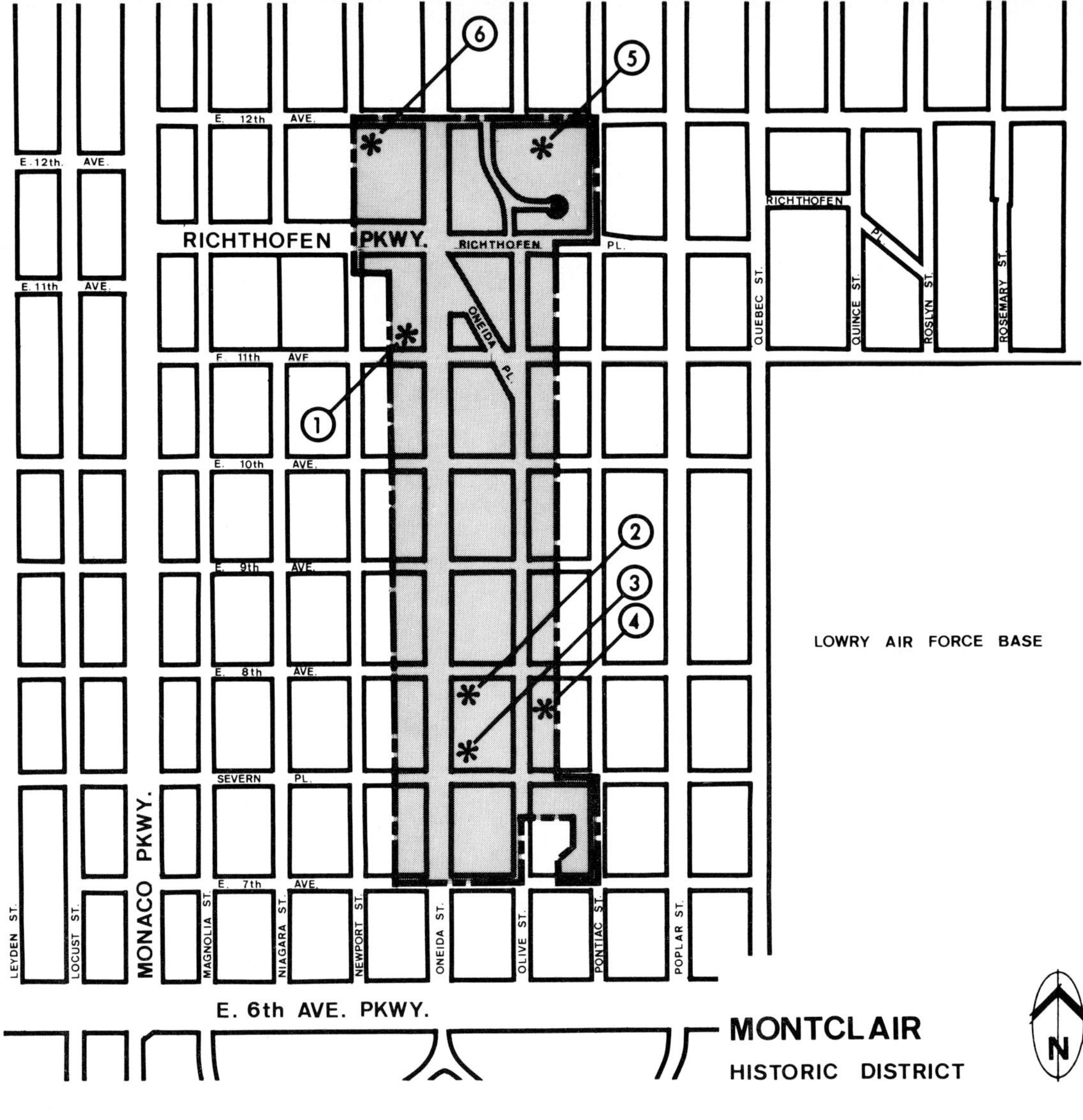
E. 12th AVE.
E.12th. AVE.
RICHTHOFEN PKWY.
RICHTHOFEN
RICHTHOFEN PL.
E. 11th AVE.
ONEIDA PL.
E. 10th AVE.
E. 9th AVE.
E. 8th AVE.
SEVERN PL.
E. 7th AVE.
E. 6th AVE. PKWY.
MONACO PKWY.
LEYDEN ST.
LOCUST ST.
MAGNOLIA ST.
NIAGARA ST.
NEWPORT ST.
ONEIDA ST.
OLIVE ST.
PONTIAC ST.
POPLAR ST.
QUEBEC ST.
QUINCE ST.
ROSLYN ST.
ROSEMARY ST.
LOWRY AIR FORCE BASE
1
2
3
4
5
6
N
MONTCLAIR
HISTORIC DISTRICT

B. Montclair Historic District

This district was originally platted in 1885 by Mathias Cochrane. He was joined by Baron Walter Von Richthofen, who expanded it and eventually took it over. A portion of "Richthofen's Montclair," as it became known, is now the Montclair Historic District. Comprising 146 properties, including the individually designated Richthofen Castle and the Montclair Civic Center, it exhibits a wide range of residential architectural styles, a few examples of which follow.

Designation Number: District 5; November 16, 1975

1. **Residence**
1101 Oneida Street

Built in 1906, the exterior was dramatically remodeled years later into the then popular Spanish Colonial Revival style. From an architectural standpoint, the renovation was extremely successful.

Montclair Historic District

2. Residence
790 Oneida Street

This modified Queen Anne style house constructed in 1892 is notable for its interesting, graceful roof lines and its fine detailing.

Montclair Historic District

3. The Pomeroy House
754 Oneida Street

Built for entrepreneur James H. Pomeroy, probably in 1898, this house was recently rescued from condemnation and extensively restored.

Montclair Historic District

4. The Mitchell-Wilfley House
770 Olive Street

Constructed in 1910 for Joseph B. Mitchell and owned for thirty-three years by the Elmer Wilfley family, it is designed in the rare (for Denver) Jacobethan style.

Montclair Historic District

5. Richthofen Castle
7020 East Twelfth Avenue

Constructed for Baron Walter Von Richthofen, it was sold to Edwin B. Hendrie in 1903 and extensively remodeled and added onto by him in 1910. Today it bears only slight resemblance to its original castle-like appearance, which was essentially Richardsonian Romanesque with prominent castellations at the roof lines.

Construction Date: *1883*
Architect: *(Original): Not known*
(Renovation): Biscoe and Benedict
Style: *Various styles*
Designation Number 32; June 11, 1973
(listed on National Register)

6. The Montclair Civic Center

6820 East Twelfth Avenue

Constructed by Baron Von Richthofen as "The Molkerei," a German-styled health spa for tuberculosis treatment, the building became an asylum for the insane in 1902. Soon forced to close because of neighborhood protest, it was acquired by the city of Denver and, in 1908, converted into the city's first community center.

Construction Date: *1898*
Architect: *Not known*
Style: *Not definable*
Designation Number 50; November 26, 1973

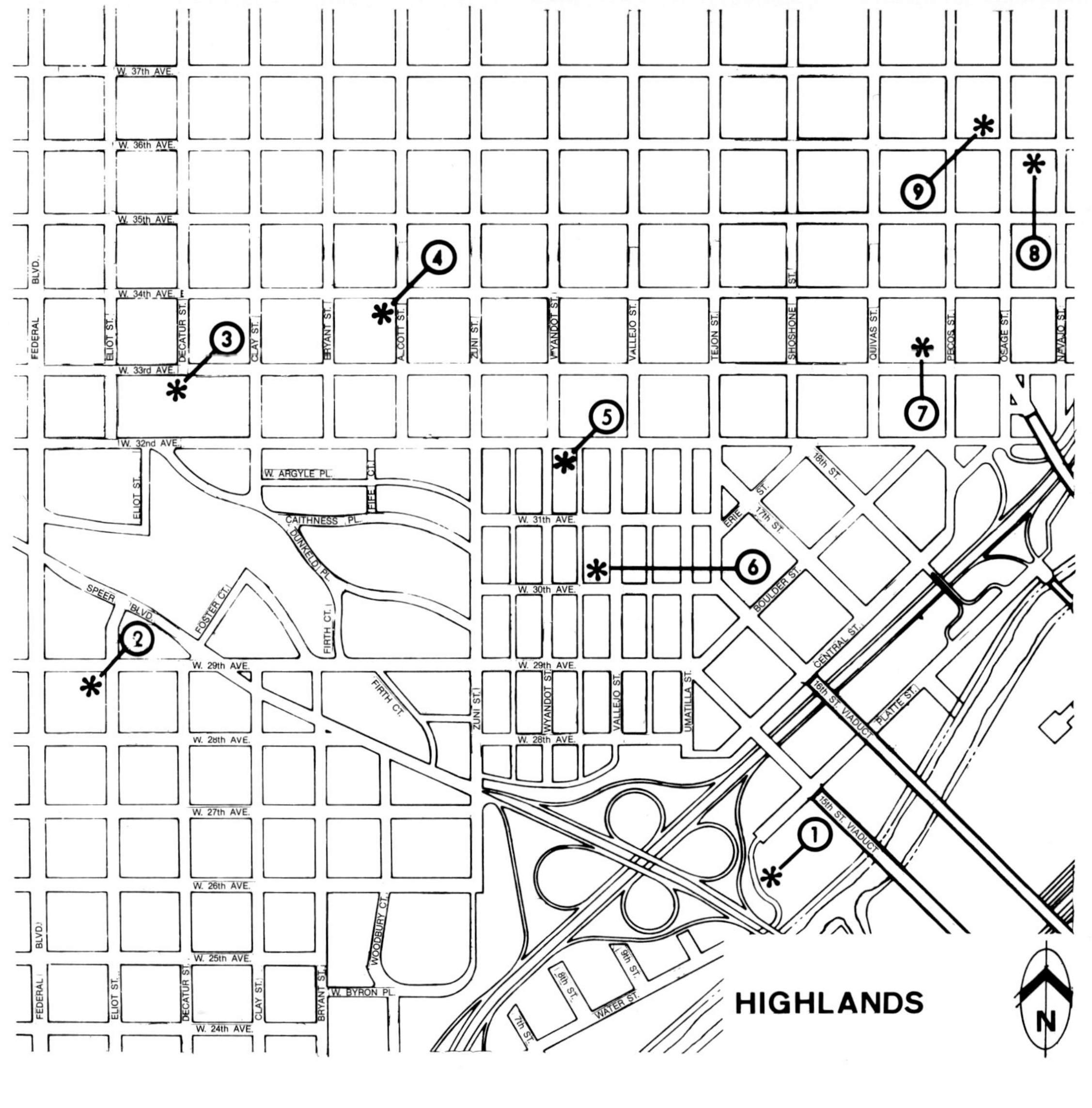
W. 37th AVE.
W. 36th AVE.
W. 35th AVE.
W. 34th AVE.
W. 33rd AVE.
W. 32nd AVE.
W. ARGYLE PL.
CAITHNESS PL.
W. 31st AVE.
W. 30th AVE.
W. 29th AVE.
W. 28th AVE.
W. 27th AVE.
W. 26th AVE.
W. 25th AVE.
W. 24th AVE.
W. BYRON PL.
FEDERAL BLVD.
ELIOT ST.
DECATUR ST.
CLAY ST.
BRYANT ST.
ALCOTT ST.
ZUNI ST.
WYANDOT ST.
VALLEJO ST.
TEJON ST.
SHOSHONE ST.
QUIVAS ST.
PECOS ST.
OSAGE ST.
NAVAJO ST.
FIFE CT.
DUNKELD PL.
FIRTH CT.
FOSTER CT.
SPEER BLVD.
UMATILLA ST.
WOODBURY CT.
ERIE ST.
18th ST.
17th ST.
BOULDER ST.
CENTRAL ST.
16th ST. VIADUCT
PLATTE ST.
15th ST. VIADUCT
9th ST.
8th ST.
7th ST.
WATER ST.
1
2
3
4
5
6
7
8
9
HIGHLANDS
N

C. Highlands

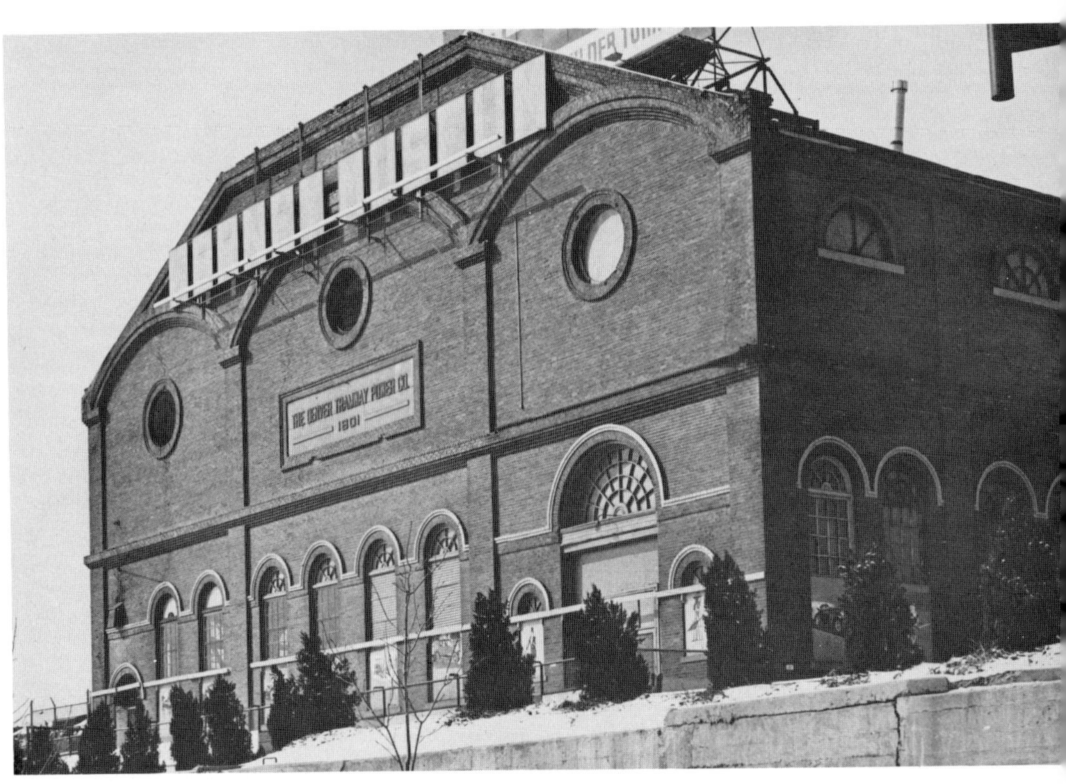
THE DENVER TRAMWAY POWER CO.
1901

1. **The Forney Transportation Museum**
1416 Platte Street

This highly visible landmark was constructed as a power plant for the Denver Tramway Power Company and now serves as a transportation museum. The architectural style was very popular with power plant engineers. In fact, the choice of this style for power plant buildings was almost mandatory, a trend that persisted well into the twentieth century.

Construction Date: *1901*
Architect: *Not known*
Style: *Modified Romanesque Revival*
Designation Number 24; May 20, 1972

2914

2. The Queree House
2914 West Twenty-ninth Avenue

This interesting small house was built—as well as designed—by the master craftsman Joseph John Queree, who was noted for his particularly fine interior woodwork.

Construction Date: *1888*
Architect: *Joseph John Queree*
Style: *Queen Anne derivative*
Designation Number 39; November 26, 1973

3. St. Elizabeth's Retreat Chapel
2825 West Thirty-second Avenue

This remarkable structure was originally part of the Oakes Home for Tubercular Patients and was acquired by the Poor Sisters of St. Francis in 1943. On two occasions it narrowly escaped demolition, and its original large open site is now closed in by buildings. An exquisitely detailed small church, its design was probably inspired by the Renaissance London churches of Christopher Wren. Its interior is exceptional.

Construction Date: *1897*
Architect: *Frederick J. Sterner*
Style: *Neoclassical Revival*
Designation Number 66; October 20, 1974
(listed on National Register)

4. The Hugh Mackay House

3359 Alcott Street

This house was constructed for Scottish emigrant Hugh Mackay, who was involved in both silver mining and construction. Built of rusticated lava stone, it displays some influence of nineteenth century Scottish domestic architecture.

Construction Date: *1891*
Architect: *Not known*
Style: *Victorian*
Designation Number 40; November 26, 1973

5. The Chapel of Our Merciful Savior
Thirty-second and Wyandot streets

Known as All Saints Episcopal Church until 1961, when a new church building was constructed for the congregation, it boasts perhaps the finest "rose" window of any Denver church of that era.

Construction Date: *1890*
Architect: *James Murdoch*
Style: *High Victorian Gothic (German)*
Designation Number 100; September 18, 1977
(listed on National Register)

6. Asbury Methodist Church

2205 West Thirtieth Avenue

Constructed as Asbury Methodist Episcopal Church, its tower is a strong visual landmark readily visible even from the Sixteenth Street shopping district. The building design is almost pure H. H. Richardson, and, in fact, owes basic design inspiration to Richardson's Trinity Church in Boston.

Construction Date: *1889*
Architect: *Kidder and Humphreys*
Style: *Richardsonian Romanesque*
Designation Number 37; November 26, 1973
(listed on National Register)

7. St. Patrick Mission Church and Rectory

3325 Pecos Street

This is the second church building of the Pioneer Catholic Parish of northwest Denver, which was established in 1883 by Bishop Machebeuf. Designed by Father Joseph P. Carrigan to resemble Franciscan missions he had visited and admired, it is now in the beginning phases of a long-range restoration process.

Construction Date: *1907*
Architect: *Father Joseph P. Carrigan*
Style: *Mission*
Designation Number 102; September 18, 1977

8. Mt. Carmel Church

3549 Navajo Street

The Mt. Carmel Parish, organized in 1894 by Father Joseph P. Carrigan to serve Italian immigrants, lost its first church building to fire in 1898. This replacement church is wonderfully evocative of the Renaissance churches of Italy. The recent exterior restoration work has done much to increase the building's attractiveness.

Construction Date: *1904*
Architect: *Not known*
Style: *Romanesque Revival (Italian)*
Designation Number 101; September 18, 1977

9. Residence

3611-3615 Osage Street

Constructed originally as his own residence by stonemason and contractor Frank Damascio, it has been used as a hospital, a convent, and an apartment house. Condemned and scheduled for demolition, it was rescued and is now being restored. Its stone facade is unusually elaborate for that period and its compelling symmetry even more rare.

Construction Date: *1895*
Architect: *Frank Damascio*
Style: *Victorian Eclectic*
Designation Number 96; February 20, 1977

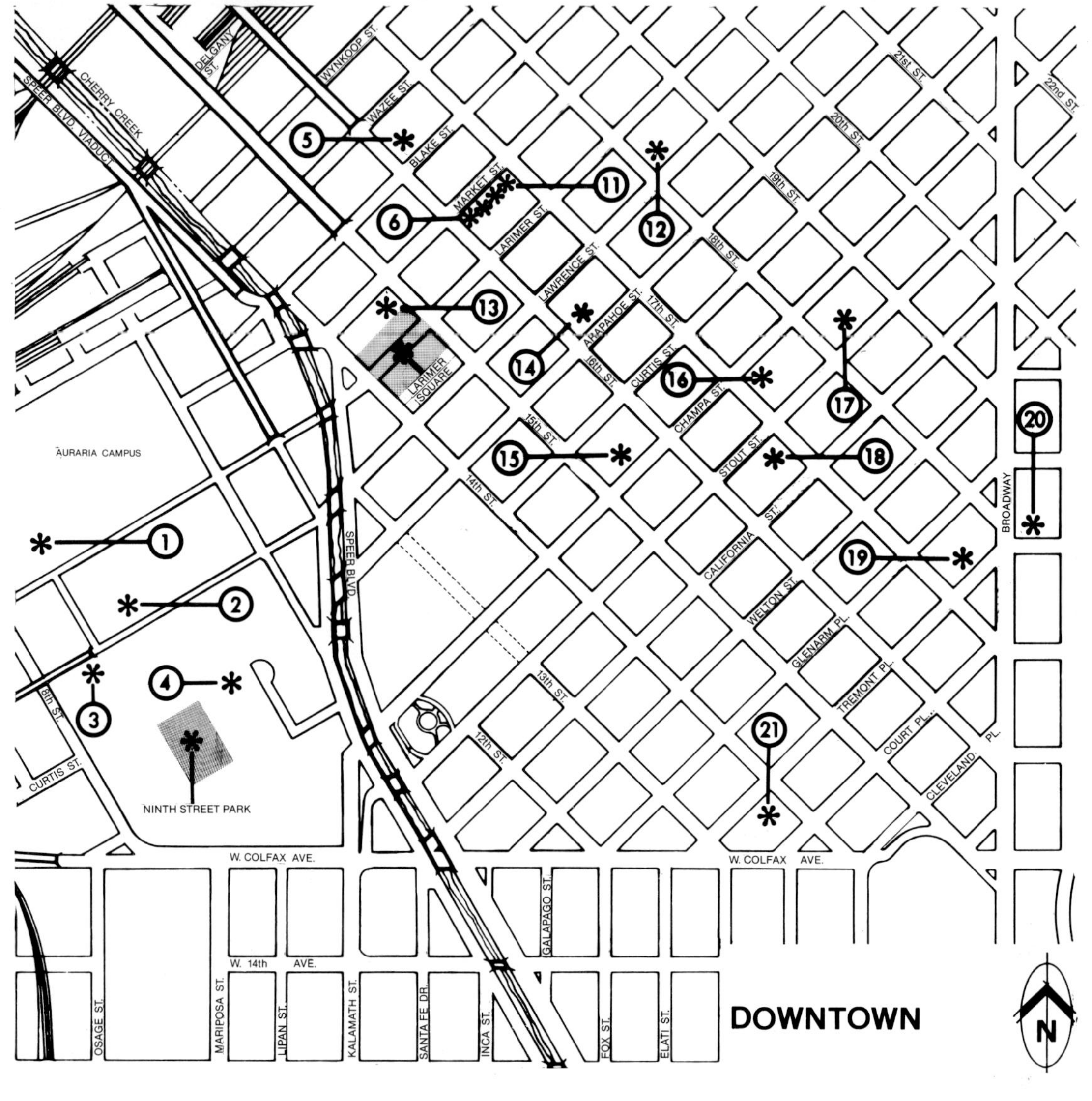
DOWNTOWN
N
WYNKOOP ST.
DELGANY ST.
WAZEE ST.
BLAKE ST.
MARKET ST.
LARIMER ST.
LAWRENCE ST.
ARAPAHOE ST.
CURTIS ST.
CHAMPA ST.
STOUT ST.
CALIFORNIA ST.
WELTON ST.
GLENARM PL.
TREMONT PL.
COURT PL.
CLEVELAND PL.
21st ST.
22nd ST.
20th ST.
19th ST.
18th ST.
17th ST.
16th ST.
15th ST.
14th ST.
13th ST.
12th ST.
CHERRY CREEK
SPEER BLVD. VIADUCT
SPEER BLVD.
LARIMER SQUARE
AURARIA CAMPUS
8th ST.
CURTIS ST.
NINTH STREET PARK
BROADWAY
W. COLFAX AVE.
W. COLFAX AVE.
W. 14th AVE.
OSAGE ST.
MARIPOSA ST.
LIPAN ST.
KALAMATH ST.
SANTA FE DR.
INCA ST.
GALAPAGO ST.
FOX ST.
ELATI ST.
1
2
3
4
5
6
11
12
13
14
15
16
17
18
19
20
21

D. Downtown

1. Tivoli Brewery
1342 Tenth Street

The main building was constructed in 1890 as the Milwaukee Brewery Company, successor to the Rocky Mountain Brewery established in the same block in 1859. The adjoining building to the south, constructed earlier (1882) as the West Denver Turn Halle, was designed by Harold W. Baerresen. The main building is a strong visual landmark, and, considering the building's functional requirement, the facade composition is outstanding.

Construction Date: *1890*
Architect: *F. C. Eberly*
Style: *Second Empire (Mansard)*
Designation Number 26; August 28, 1972
(listed on National Register)

2. Emmanuel-Sherith Israel Chapel

1201 Tenth Street (Auraria Campus)

Denver's oldest surviving church building was originally Emmanuel Episcopal Chapel, constructed on the site of the first Sunday school in the Rocky Mountain region. In 1902, it was acquired by the congregation Sherith Israel and converted to a synagogue.

Now, as part of the Auraria campus, it is used as an art gallery.

Construction Date: *1876*
Architect: *Not known*
Style: *High Victorian Gothic*
Designation Number 3; January 9, 1968
(listed on National Register)

3. St. Cajetan's Church
Ninth and Lawrence streets

This church, now part of the Auraria Higher Education Center, was constructed on the homestead of early Denver businessman John K. Mullen, who also donated $50,000 toward its construction.

Construction Date: *1926*
Architect: *R. Willison*
Style: *Spanish Colonial Revival*
Designation Number 19; April 4, 1970
(listed on National Register)

4. St. Elizabeth's Church

1060 Eleventh Street (Auraria Campus)

The first Catholic Church in Colorado to be consecrated, it was built on the site of an earlier church erected to serve St. Elizabeth's Parish. The chancel on the west side of the building is a particularly attractive design element, characteristic of a style popular some forty years earlier.

Construction Date: *1898*
Architect: *Father Adrian, O.F.M.*
Style: *Romanesque Revival*
Designation Number 14; April 19, 1969
(listed on National Register)

TWO
WAY
TRAFFIC

5. Constitution Hall

1507 Blake Street

The first permanent home of the First National Bank of Colorado, its name derives from having housed the Colorado Constitutional Convention during 1875-76. Among its early owners were Edward M. McCook, territorial governor of Colorado and later appointed minister to Hawaii, and Eben Smith, Colorado miner, railroader, and banker.

On April 24, 1977, it suffered a disastrous fire and little remains beyond the Blake Street facade.

Construction Date: *1865*
(The third floor, added later, gave it its distinguishing architectural style.)
Architect: *Not known*
Style: *Second Empire (Mansard)*
Designation Number 2; January 9, 1968
(listed on National Register)

BLK
LEASE
477-6070
1620

6. The Hitchings Block
1620 Market Street

The first of a group of six designated landmarks in the sixteen hundred block of Market Street, it was built for the Reverend Horace Baldwin Hitchings, who came to Denver in 1862 to be the minister of St. John's in the Wilderness, an Episcopalian parish that eventually built St. John's Cathedral.

Construction Date: *1892*
Architect: *Not known*
Style: *Victorian Commercial*
Designation Number 59; June 17, 1974

1624

7. **The Liebhardt-Lindner Building**
1624 Market Street

Constructed for Gustavus Liebhardt to house his wholesale fruit company, it has recently been renovated for use as commercial and office space. Liebhardt was well-known as the developer of the once-famous Rose Gardens in Edgewater (now Lakewood).

Construction Date: *1881*
Architect: *Not known*
Style: *Victorian Commercial*
Designation Number 60; June 17, 1974

8. The McCrary Building

1634 Market Street

One of the most attractive of the six designated buildings in the area, its facade was completely remodeled sometime around 1905. Built for Thomas B. McCrary to house his wholesale grocery business, it continued in that use until 1905, when McCrary became vice-president of the Merchants Insurance Company.

Construction Date: *1884*
Architect: *Not known*
Style: *Commercial*
Designation Number 61; June 17, 1974

9. **Commercial Building**
1642 Market Street

Little is known of this building's early history beyond that it was constructed on land purchased by Angeline C. Yard for $105. Recently renovated, it now serves for commercial and office use.

Construction Date: *1885*
Architect: *Not known*
Style: *Victorian Commercial*
Designation Number 62; June 17, 1974

10. Commercial Building

1644 Market Street

Constructed by William R. Gorsline, it was later sold to Charles B. Kountze, one of the founders of the Colorado National Bank. In all probability it at one time had a large stamped-tin cornice.

Construction Date: *1884*
Architect: *Not known*
Style: *Victorian Commercial*
Designation Number 63; June 17, 1974

THE COLUMBIA
HOTEL
STATE BARBER COLLEGES
Ranchers-Farmers-Sheepmen
EMPLOYMENT SERVICE
COLUMBIA
HOTEL
COLUMBIA
GRILL

11. The Columbia Hotel Building

1322 Seventeenth Street

The largest—as well as the oldest—of this Market Street group, it was originally constructed as a commercial building but was converted to hotel use in 1892.

Construction Date: *Circa 1872*
Architect: *Not known*
Style: *Victorian Commercial*
Designation Number 64; June 17, 1974

DENVER CITY CABLE RAILWAY CO
the old spaghetti factory

12. The Tramway Cable Building

1801 Lawrence Street

Constructed by the Denver City Cable Railway Company to provide power for the cable car system, it was purchased in 1899 by the Denver Tramway Company, which converted the system for overhead electric trolley use.

(See also: Forney Transportation Museum.)

Construction Date: *1889*
Architect: *Not known*
Style: *Modified Romanesque Revival*
Designation Number 30; January 22, 1973
(listed on National Register)

LIFE
CYCLE

13. The Wells Fargo Building
Fifteenth and Market streets

This structure was built by Wells Fargo on the site of the original 1866 Wells Fargo Company Building. Sometime after World War II, the upper two of the three stories were condemned and demolished.

Construction Date: *1874*
Architect: *Not known*
Style: *High Victorian Gothic*
Designation Number 109; October 22, 1978

15. Odd Fellows Hall
1545 Champa Street

Built for the Odd Fellows, who have continuously occupied the upper floors since construction of the building, it was known as a gathering place for early Denver jazz musicians. Except for the large stained-glass window, the design elements, particularly the stamped tin cornices, are fairly typical of the commercial construction of the 1880s.

Construction Date: *1887*
Architect: *Not known*
Style: *Victorian Commercial*
Designation Number 31; January 22, 1973

NO DOUBLE TURN
ONLY

16. The Colorado Federal Building

821 Seventeenth Street

Constructed by the Dome Investment Company, a holding company of Claude Boettcher and F. A. Bonfils, it was originally called the Ideal Building. The first reinforced concrete multistory structure constructed west of the Mississippi River, it was extensively remodeled in 1924 by architects William and Arthur Fisher.

Construction Date: *1907*
Architects: *Montana Fallis and John Stein*
Style: *Commercial*
Designation Number 105; November 13, 1977
(listed on National Register)

17. United States Post Office Building
Eighteenth and Stout streets

Constructed in a monumental scale of Colorado yule marble, it remains Denver's major structure of classical design.

Construction Date: *1910*
Architect: *Tracy, Swarthwout, and Litchfield*
(See also: St. John's Cathedral.)
Style: *Neoclassical Revival*
Designation Number 65; August 26, 1974
(listed on National Register)

18. The Equitable Building
730 Seventeenth Street

A distinguished Denver landmark, it was erected to be the western headquarters of the Equitable Assurance Company of New York and is credited with stimulating commercial construction on Seventeenth Street. Its architectural style, while unique to Denver, was popular at the time in eastern cities. The lobby is particularly noteworthy.

Under the aegis of its new owners,
the building exterior is being largely restored.

Construction Date: *1892*
Architect: *Andrews, Jacques, and Rantoul*
Style: *Second Renaissance Revival*
Designation Number 103; September 18, 1977
(listed on National Register)

THE
NAVARRE
1880

19. The Old Navarre Restaurant

1727 Tremont Place

Originally the Brinker Collegiate Institute, a Christian college, in 1889 it was renovated as the Richelieu Hotel, a notorious gambling house and bordello. In 1914 it became the Navarre Cafe and has continued as a restaurant, although somewhat intermittently in recent times.

Construction Date: *1880*
Architect: *Not known*
Style: *Victorian Bracketed*
Designation Number 21; November 27, 1971
(listed on National Register)

20. Trinity Methodist Church

1820 Broadway

Constructed under the direction of its great pastor, Henry A. Buchtel, who also served as a governor of Colorado and as a chancellor of the University of Denver, the church was known originally as Trinity Methodist Episcopal Church (see cornerstone). It has an unusual lava stone spire and a large stained-glass window designed by Tiffany.

Construction Date: *1888*
Architect: *Robert S. Roeschlaub*
Style: *High Victorian Gothic*
Designation Number 6; April 27, 1968
(listed on National Register)

D.F.D
No. 1.
DENVER FIRE DEPARTMENT
MUSEUM
1326

21. Fire Station Number One

1326 Tremont Place

Although not the first of Denver's many fire stations, it became the home of Engine Company Number One upon its completion in 1909. While removal of the entrance canopy and new doors have somewhat altered its original appearance, the facade retains considerable architectural vigor. The building will serve as a museum for the Denver Fire Department.

Construction Date: *1909*
Architect: *G. W. Huntington and Company*
Style: *Second Renaissance Revival*
Designation Number 53; February 2, 1974

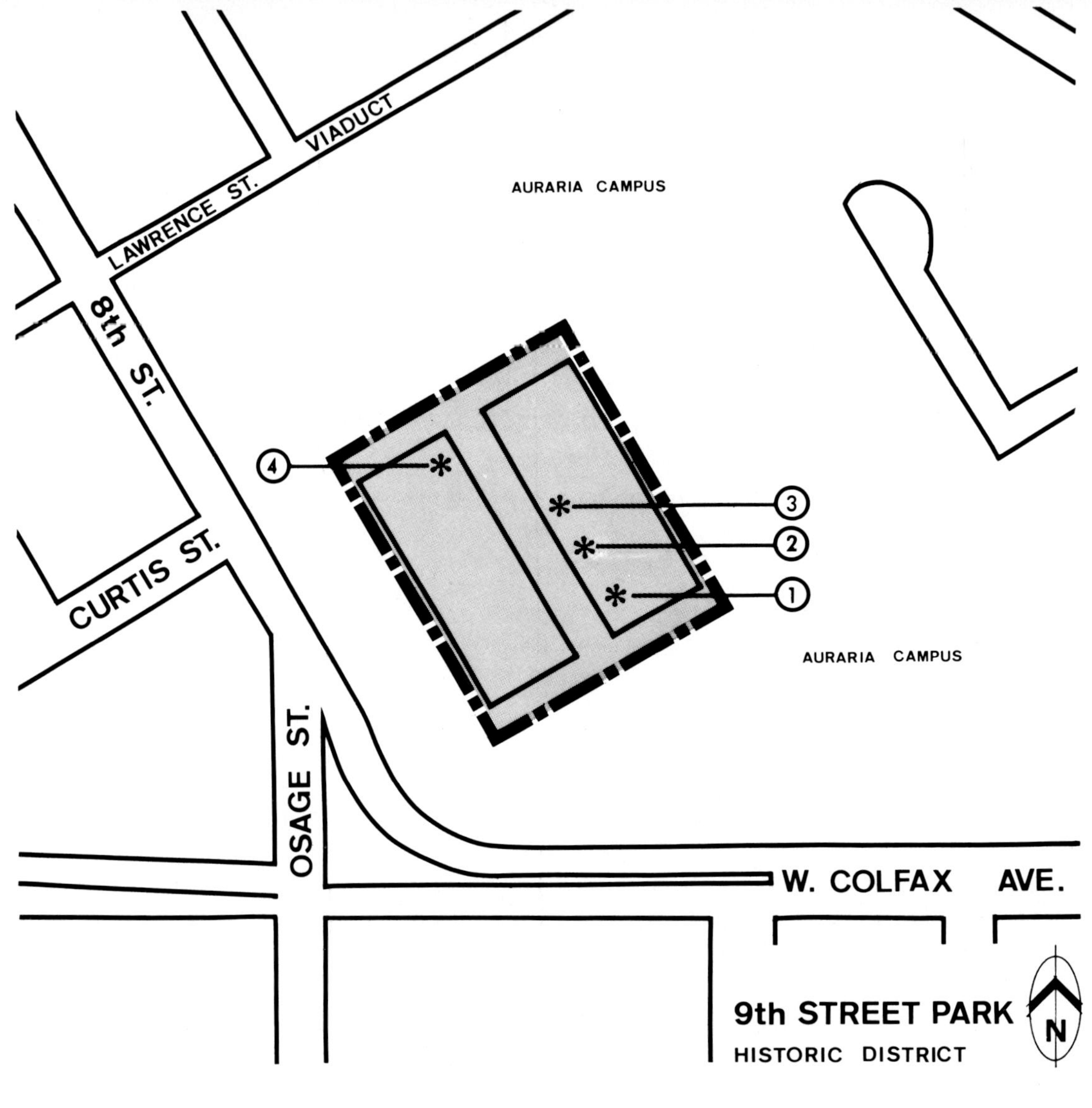
VIADUCT
LAWRENCE ST.
AURARIA CAMPUS
8th ST.
CURTIS ST.
4
3
2
1
AURARIA CAMPUS
OSAGE ST.
W. COLFAX AVE.
9th STREET PARK
HISTORIC DISTRICT
N

E. The Ninth Street Historic District

Auraria Campus

This remarkably diverse group of houses, built in the 1870s and '80s, is now utilized as offices for various campus functions. Acquired by DURA, Ninth Street was saved from demolition and completely restored through the heroic efforts of Historic Denver, Inc. The thirteen houses and one commercial structure comprising the district represent a cross section of early Denver residential styles.

Designation Number: District 3; June 11, 1973
(listed on National Register)

1. **The Stephen Knight House**
1015 Ninth Street

Built in 1885 by Charles Davis for his daughter, Annie Kate, and son-in-law, Stephen Knight, it is a finely executed example of the Second Empire style.

Ninth Street Park Historic District

2. The John E. Witte House
1027 Ninth Street

Constructed, also in the Second Empire style, in 1883, it boasts a charming tower, which sets off the entrance. After 1898 it was occupied by the John E. Witte family.

Ninth Street Park Historic District

3. The Jeremiah Gardner House
1033 Ninth Street

Reminiscent of the Italian Villa style, this delightful house was built in 1873 for and by carpenter Jeremiah Gardner, who also built the house next door, number 1027.

Ninth Street Park Historic District

4. The Charles Davis R. House
1068 Ninth Street

Mill owner Charles R. Davis built this Italianate style house after he arrived here from Illinois in 1870. The wood detailing of the front porch is exceptionally fine for a house of this modest size.

Ninth Street Park Historic District

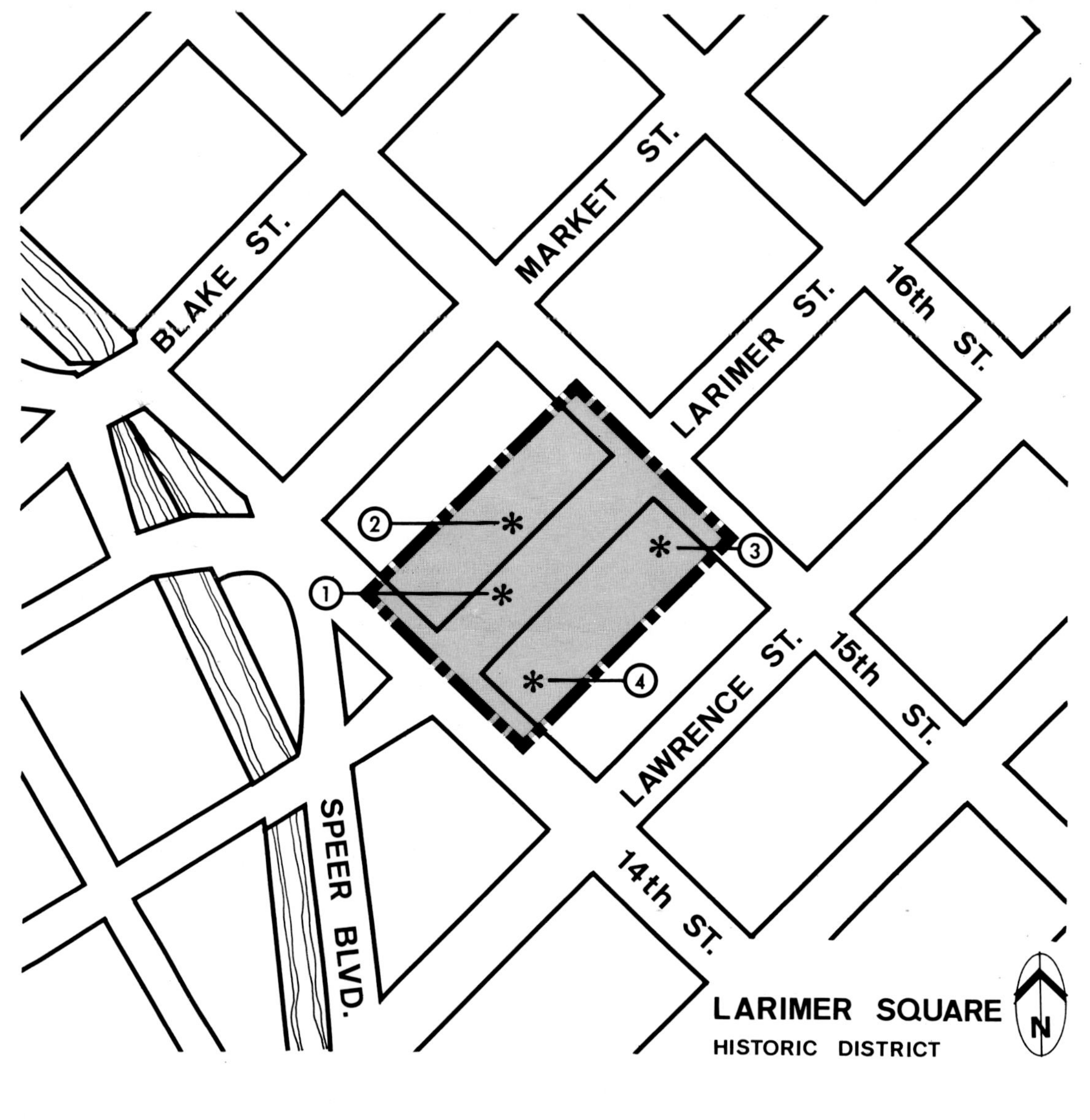
BLAKE ST.
MARKET ST.
LARIMER ST.
16th ST.
LAWRENCE ST.
15th ST.
14th ST.
SPEER BLVD.
1
2
3
4
N
LARIMER SQUARE
HISTORIC DISTRICT

F. The Larimer Square Historic District

The first area to receive historic district designation in Denver, it occupies the two half blocks where Denver had its beginning in 1858. Denver's rapid growth soon forced demolition of the original buildings and their replacement with larger, more permanent structures. The seventeen commercial structures comprising the district, all constructed between 1870 and 1890, are typical examples of the styles of that period.

Following the silver crash of 1893, this original downtown was replaced by Denver's new "uptown" downtown, and the area rapidly declined. By 1964, when the Larimer Square project was started, this was an area of derelict structures supporting only marginal businesses and empty buildings.

Designed by architect Langdon Morris, Larimer Square is an early and classic example of the concept of preservation through adaptive reuse, the process of renovating—rather than restoring—old structures into economically viable contemporary uses.

Designation Number: District 1; July 31, 1971
(listed on National Register)

1. View of the Northwest Side of Larimer Square

The variety in commercial architectural styles popular in Denver during the 1870s and 1880s is exemplified here.

Larimer Square Historic District

2. Commercial Building
1439 Larimer Square

This decorative 1875 building exhibits considerably more detail than other Larimer Square buildings. The excellent cast-iron first-story columns (manufactured by the Union Foundry in Chicago) provide an interesting contrast to the overscaled window heads and cornice (stamped-tin catalog items).

Larimer Square Historic District

the stitchin post
Exhibit b ltd.

3. The Keep Courtyard

One of the spaces created by selective demolition of additions to the original building, it serves to open up the interior of the square.

Larimer Square Historic District

4. The Courtyard of the Bull and Bear

The area was so named because of the carved stone bull and bear, which were rescued from the old Mining Exchange Building and incorporated into the archway through the Sussex Building. This open space was also created by demolishing later additions to original buildings.

Larimer Square Historic District

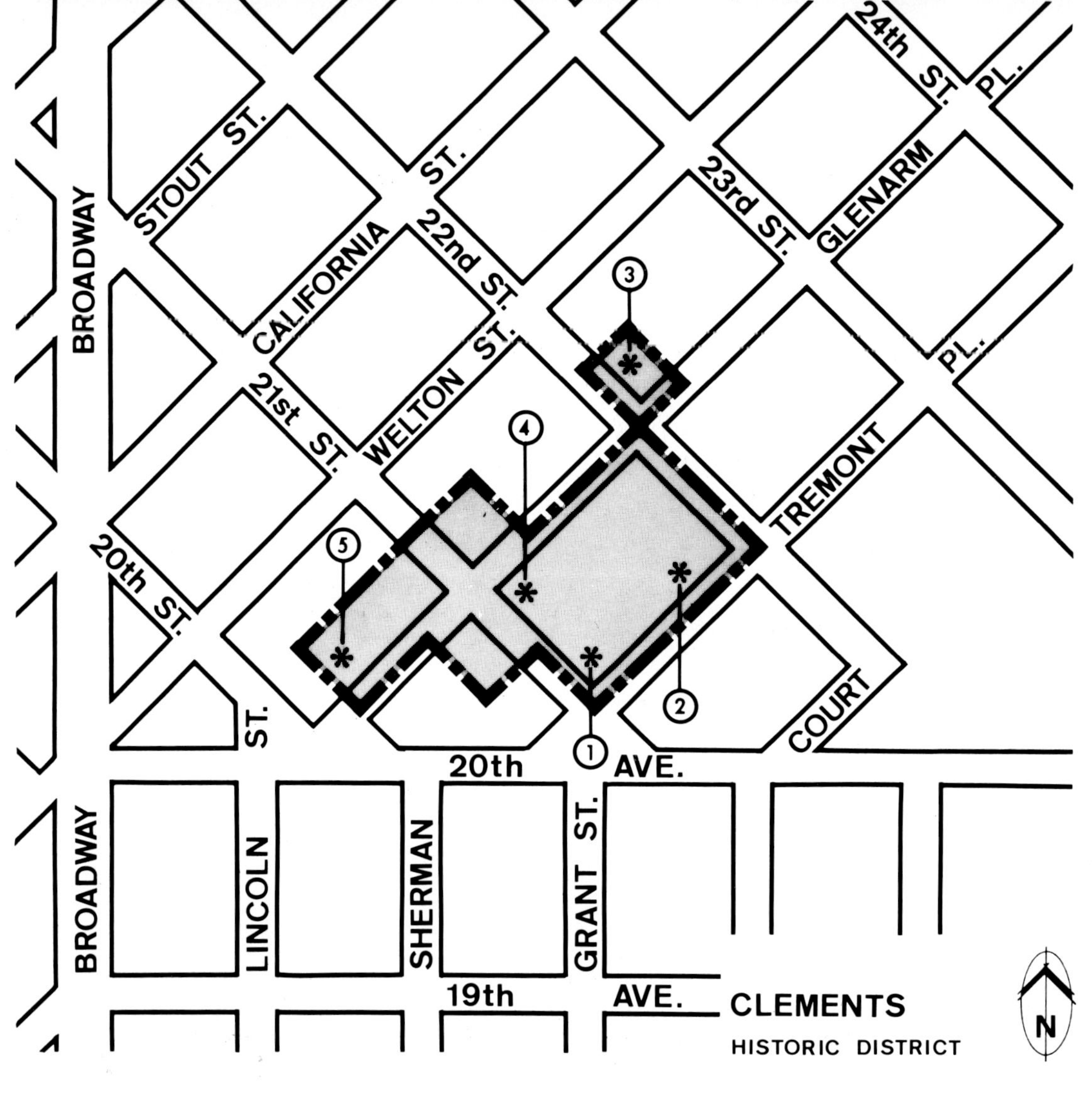
BROADWAY
STOUT ST.
CALIFORNIA ST.
WELTON ST.
GLENARM PL.
TREMONT PL.
COURT PL.
20th ST.
21st ST.
22nd ST.
23rd ST.
24th ST.
20th AVE.
19th AVE.
LINCOLN ST.
SHERMAN
GRANT ST.
1
2
3
4
5
N
CLEMENTS
HISTORIC DISTRICT

G. The Clements Historic District

This interesting residential district, which includes the individually designated St. Andrew's Memorial Church, has experienced a remarkable renaissance in the four years since its designation. Deteriorated, run-down, and partially slum, its houses have been purchased for their own use by young management and professional families and substantially restored—a classic example of core city revitalization. Part of Alfred Clements' Denver Addition, most of these houses were built between 1871 and 1890 for prominent early Denver citizens. On the following pages are shown some of the finest of these historic district structures.

Designation Number: District 4; August 23, 1975

TREMONT

1. The Kingston
Twenty-first Street and Tremont Place

Designed and built in 1890 by Arthur S. Miller, who because of his activities in the field was known as "Apartment House Miller," this building originally consisted of six rowhouses. Eventually converted to twenty-one apartments, it is now in the process of restoration and conversion back to rowhouses. Its pleasantly undulating Queen Anne facade is somewhat marred by the harsh and unpleasant color scheme—purported to be historically accurate, more's the pity.

Clements Historic District

2. The DeWitt Roberts House
2151 Tremont Place

This house was built in 1886 by DeWitt Roberts, principal of the Broadway School and then of the Ebert School. He was later one of the founders and incorporators of the town of Ordway, Colorado. The classic Queen Anne style of this charming building has been considerably enhanced by its recent restoration.

Clements Historic District

3. Row Houses

Twenty-Second Street and Glenarm Place

Now undergoing restoration and renovation back to their original function, when built in 1884 they were the classic example of adaptation of the High Victorian Italianate style to modest row houses.

Clements Historic District

4 HOUR
PARKING
8AM 6PM
NO
PARKING
ANY
TIME

4. The Hugh H. Thomas House

2104 Glenarm Place

This outstanding house was constructed in 1883 for Hugh H. Thomas, who was, with George A. Gano, a partner in the furniture company Gano & Thomas.

The house is a rare surviving example of the work of noted early Colorado architect William Quayle and displays his characteristic unusual detailing. The general elements are Victorian, of course, but more Quayle than any recognized style.

Clements Historic District
(listed on National Register)

St. Andrew's
ABBEY

5. St. Andrew's Memorial Church (St. Andrew's Abbey)
2015 Glenarm Place

This small, intimate church was commissioned by A. Dupont Parker as a memorial to his wife. The only known Colorado work of the great American architect Ralph Adams Cram, it bears some resemblance to his St. George's Chapel in Newport, Rhode Island, although considerably smaller. The interior is particularly distinguished, due in part to recent renovation work by the Order of the Holy Family.

Construction Date: *1909*
Architect: *Ralph Adams Cram*
Style: *Late Gothic Revival*
Designation Number 67; October 20, 1974
(listed on National Register)

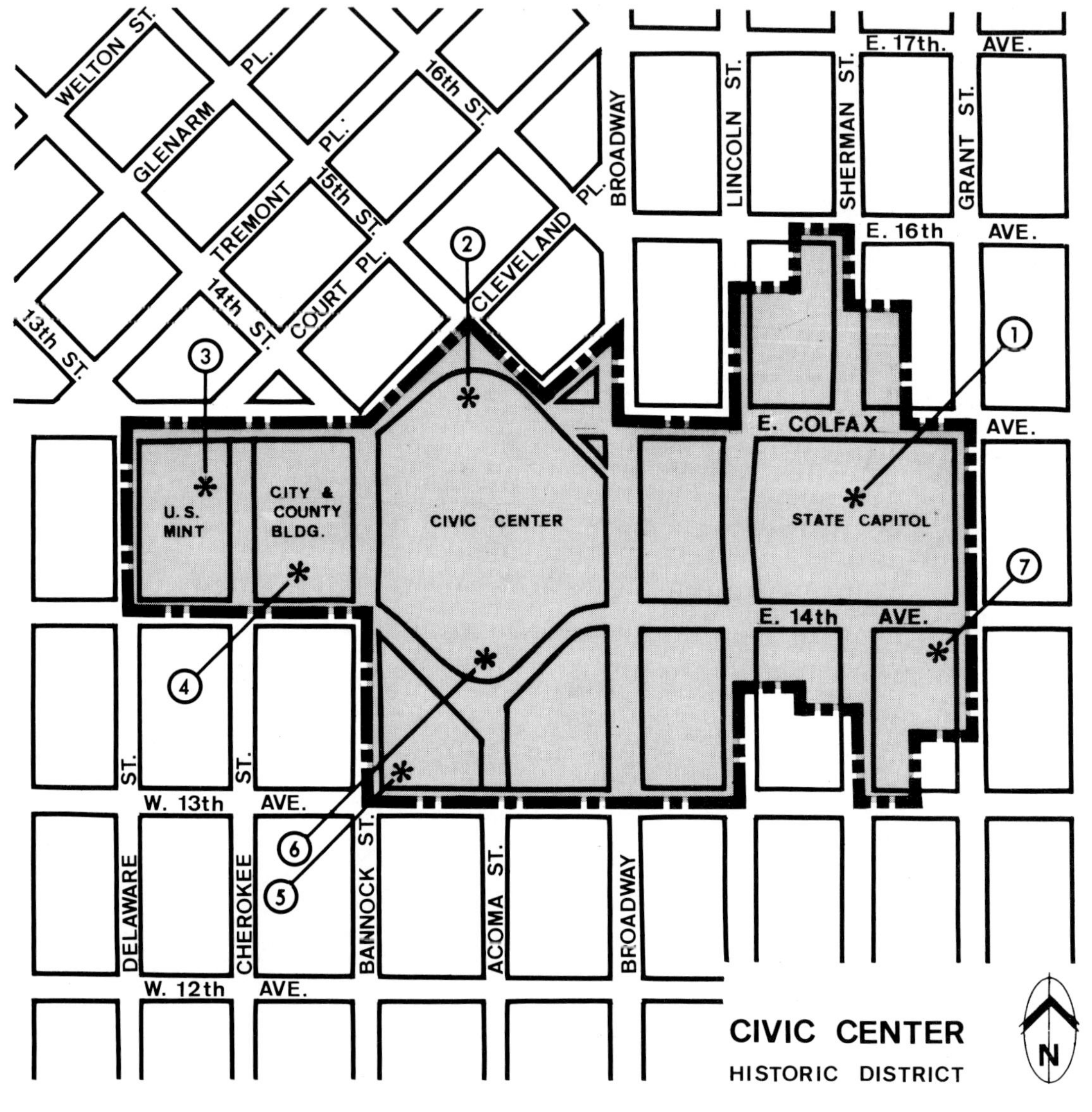
WELTON ST.
PL.
16th ST.
GLENARM
PL.
15th ST.
TREMONT
COURT PL.
14th ST.
13th ST.
CLEVELAND
PL.
BROADWAY
LINCOLN ST.
SHERMAN ST.
GRANT ST.
E. 17th. AVE.
E. 16th AVE.
E. COLFAX AVE.
E. 14th AVE.
U. S. MINT
CITY & COUNTY BLDG.
CIVIC CENTER
STATE CAPITOL
W. 13th AVE.
W. 12th AVE.
DELAWARE ST.
CHEROKEE ST.
BANNOCK ST.
ACOMA ST.
BROADWAY
1
2
3
4
5
6
7
N
CIVIC CENTER
HISTORIC DISTRICT

H. The Civic Center Historic District

Extending irregularly from Grant Street west to Delaware Street and from Colfax Avenue south to Thirteenth Avenue, the district contains most of the major administrative and cultural buildings of both the state and city. The concept of the Civic Center was proposed in 1904 by Henry Read, and its final development was established and initiated by Mayor Robert. W. Speer during his last term of office (1916-19). Included in the district are the individually designated U.S. Mint and the First Baptist Church, as well as the State Capitol, the City and County Building, the Judicial-Heritage Center, the Denver Public Library, the Voorhies Memorial Gateway, and other noteworthy buildings, monuments, and statues.

Designation Number: District 6; April 23, 1976

1. The Colorado State Capitol Building
East Fourteenth Avenue and Lincoln Street

Dominating the Civic Center with its gold-plated dome and massive walls of gray granite, the Capitol was designed by Elijah E. Myers (Detroit, Michigan), and its construction was supervised by Denver architect Frank E. Edbrooke. Designed in the Second Renaissance Revival style, its Greek cross plan has four similar facades, each symmetrical. The cornerstone was laid in 1890. Although all of the exterior wall granite came from the same quarries near Gunnison, Colorado, the granite of the central tower, which supports the dome, is quite different in color.

Civic Center Historic District

BOOKS

2. The Voorhies Memorial Gateway
West Colfax Avenue and Cheyenne Place

Designed by architects William E. and Arthur A. Fisher and constructed in 1921, this elegant Neoclassical Revival style colonnade was constructed as a memorial to John H. P. Voorhies, a prominent early Denver resident. The structure counterpoints and balances the Greek Theater, located on the south side of the Center.

Civic Center Historic District

3. The Denver United States Mint

320 West Colfax Avenue

Although established in 1862 by an act of Congress, it operated until 1904 at Sixteenth and Market streets in the facility acquired in 1863 from the private mint of Clark, Gruber & Company. The design inspiration for the mint was obviously the fifteenth century Florentine palazzi Riccardi and Strozzi.

Construction Date: *1897*
Architect: *James Knox Taylor*
Style: *Second Renaissance Revival*
Designation Number 28; August 28, 1972
(listed on National Register)

4. The Denver City and County Building

1437 Bannock Street

Constructed in 1932 in the Neoclassical Revival style, its design was the result of a collaboration of thirty-nine Denver architects who called themselves the Allied Architects Association, of which architect Robert K. Fuller was the president.

Civic Center Historic District

5. The Evans House
1310 Bannock Street

Built by William W. Byers, publisher of the Rocky Mountain News, *the house was purchased in 1890 by William Grey Evans, who was the son of John Evans, the second territorial governor of Colorado (1861) and an important leader in the early development of Colorado.*

(See also: Evans Memorial Chapel and Governor's Mansion.)

Construction Date: *1880*
Architect: *Not known*
Style: *Victorian Eclectic*
Designation Number 5; April 27, 1968
(listed on National Register)

6. The Greek Theater
West Fourteenth Avenue and Acoma Street

A classic example of structures built throughout the United States in the "City Beautiful" era, it provides seating for 1200 around its open stage. Designed by architects Marean and Norton in the Neoclassical Revival style, it was constructed in 1919.

Civic Center Historic District

7. The First Baptist Church

East Fourteenth Avenue and Grant Street

A stylistic throwback to the James Gibbs churches of Renaissance London via Atlantic seaboard Georgian antecedents, this structure was given landmark designation when it was barely thirty years old. It is an outstanding example of an architectural style rarely utilized for churches in this region.

Construction Date: *1938*
Architect: *G. Meredith Musick*
Style: *Georgian Revival*
Designation Number 8; September 28, 1968

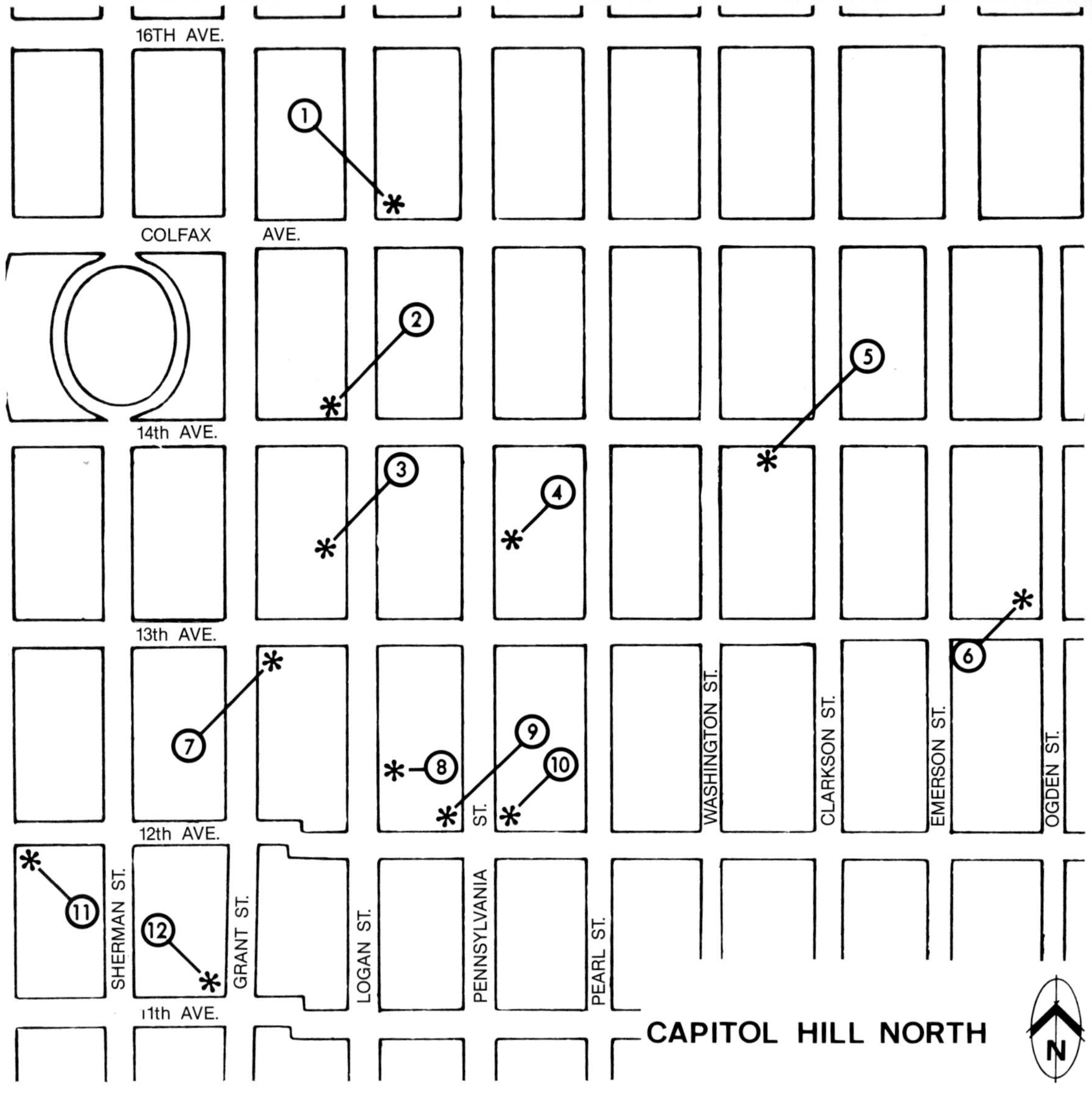
16TH AVE.
COLFAX AVE.
14th AVE.
13th AVE.
12th AVE.
11th AVE.
SHERMAN ST.
GRANT ST.
LOGAN ST.
PENNSYLVANIA ST.
PEARL ST.
WASHINGTON ST.
CLARKSON ST.
EMERSON ST.
OGDEN ST.
1
2
3
4
5
6
7
8
9
10
11
12
CAPITOL HILL NORTH
N

I. Capitol Hill North

1. The Cathedral of the Immaculate Conception
301 East Colfax Avenue

An outstanding example of French Gothic architecture in the United States, it contains 36 German-made stained-glass windows and a nave area that soars 90 feet to a vaulted ceiling. Much of its fine original interior has been modernized in recent years.

Construction Date: *1902*
Architect: *Leon Coguard*
Style: *Late Gothic Revival (French)*
Designation Number 4; April 27, 1968
(listed on National Register)

THE ETERNAL GOD IS THY REFVGE

2. The First Church of Christ Scientist
1401 Logan Street

This imposing structure constructed of white lava stone from Salida is notable for its large dome-shaped roof and colonnaded portico. The architectural detailing, predominantly in the Ionic style, is beautifully executed.

Construction Date: *1901*
Architect: *Frederick J. Sterner*
Style: *Neoclassical Revival*
Designation Number 9; September 28, 1968

3. The Denver Woman's Press Club
1325 Logan Street

This was originally a studio-home constructed for George Elbert Burr, a noted artist considered to be America's foremost etcher of nature subjects. In 1924 it was purchased for use as the Denver Woman's Press Club, a nonprofit organization founded in 1898.

Construction Date: *1910*
Architect: *Varian and Varian*
Style: *Eclectic*
Designation Number 11; December 21, 1968

4. The Molly Brown House (House of Lions)

1340 Pennsylvania Street

Started in 1887, the house was purchased in 1894 by mining magnate James Joseph Brown, who was a recognized mining expert and part owner of the Little Jonny Mine in Leadville, one the the richest gold mines in history. Known originally as the "House of Lions," it became nationally famous because of the popular musical play and movie The Unsinkable Molly Brown, *which depicted the colorful life of Margaret (Maggie) Brown. On the brink of demolition, it was acquired and restored by Historic Denver, Inc., and now serves as a museum.*

Construction Date: *1887-1889*
Architect: *William Lang*
Style: *Victorian*
Designation Number 20; March 20, 1971
(listed on National Register)

5. St. John's Cathedral

1313 Clarkson Street

This masterpiece building was the final in a series of churches of a pioneer local congregation, the First Episcopal Parish, which was established in 1859 and chartered in 1861 as St. John's in the Wilderness. A national architectural competition for its design was won by the New York firm of Tracy and Swarthwout over a field of distinguished architects, including the great Ralph Adams Cram.

Although Gothic in style, it retains the strong elements and solidity of its Romanesque antecedents.

Construction Date: *1911*
Architect: *Tracy and Swarthwout*
Style: *Late Gothic Revival (English)*
Designation Number 7; April 27, 1968
(listed on National Register)

6. The Cornwall

921 East Thirteenth Avenue

Constructed for real estate developer W. T. Cornwall, it is perhaps the earliest Denver building exhibiting elements of the Spanish Colonial style (although other stylistic details are incorporated into its fanciful facades). It has been recently restored and renovated into condominium units.

Construction Date: *1901*
Architect: *Walter Rice (an engineer)*
Style: *Eclectic*
Designation Number 91; May 23, 1976
(listed on National Register)

7. The Creswell House

1244 Grant Street

This house was constructed for Joseph Creswell, a prominent Denver manufacturer.

Construction Date: *1889*
Architect: *John J. Huddart*
Style: *Richardsonian Romanesque*
Designation Number 84; September 28, 1975
(listed on National Register)

8. Residence
1208 Logan Street

This charming small house, known as one of the "Logan Street Cottages," is considered the last frame house on Capitol Hill. (The bay window is not original.)

Construction Date: *1886*
Architect: *Not known*
Style: *Victorian (builder vernacular)*
Designation Number 90; April 18, 1976

PENNSYLVANIA
12

9. **Residence**
1207 Pennsylvania Street

The home of several prominent early Denver families, it displays the specific elements characteristic of its architectural style—in spite of the minimal number of round-arched windows.

Construction Date: *1892*
Architect: *Reiche, Carter, and Smith*
Style: *Richardsonian Romanesque*
Designation Number 80; July 6, 1975

10. Residence

1200 Pennsylvania Street

Constructed for prominent Denver real estate businessman Walter Dunning, it was subsequently purchased by State Supreme Court Justice Mitchell Benedict. The house is perhaps the finest of Denver landmarks exemplifying the Richardsonian Romanesque style.

(See also: Raymond House.)

Construction Date: *1889*
Architect: *William Lang*
Style: *Richardsonian Romanesque*
Designation Number 79; July 6, 1975

11. St. Mark's Church
1160 Lincoln Street

Much of this church's design strength was lost when all but the base of its stone bell tower had to be removed because of serious structural damage basically due to the soft sandstone material utilized in its construction.

Construction Date: *1890*
Architect: *Lang and Pugh*
Style: *Victorian Gothic Eclectic*
Designation Number 17; February 14, 1970
(listed on National Register)

12. The Dennis Sheedy House

1115 Grant Street

This house was constructed for Dennis Sheedy, who, starting out penniless, became extremely wealthy through mining, cattle, and banking and mercantile interests. Although not distinguished architecturally in spite of its imposing size, it is notable for its fine interior woodwork, executed by the master craftsman Joseph John Queree.

Construction Date: *1892*
Architect: *E. T. Carr*
Style: *Queen Anne*
Designation Number 52; January 19, 1974

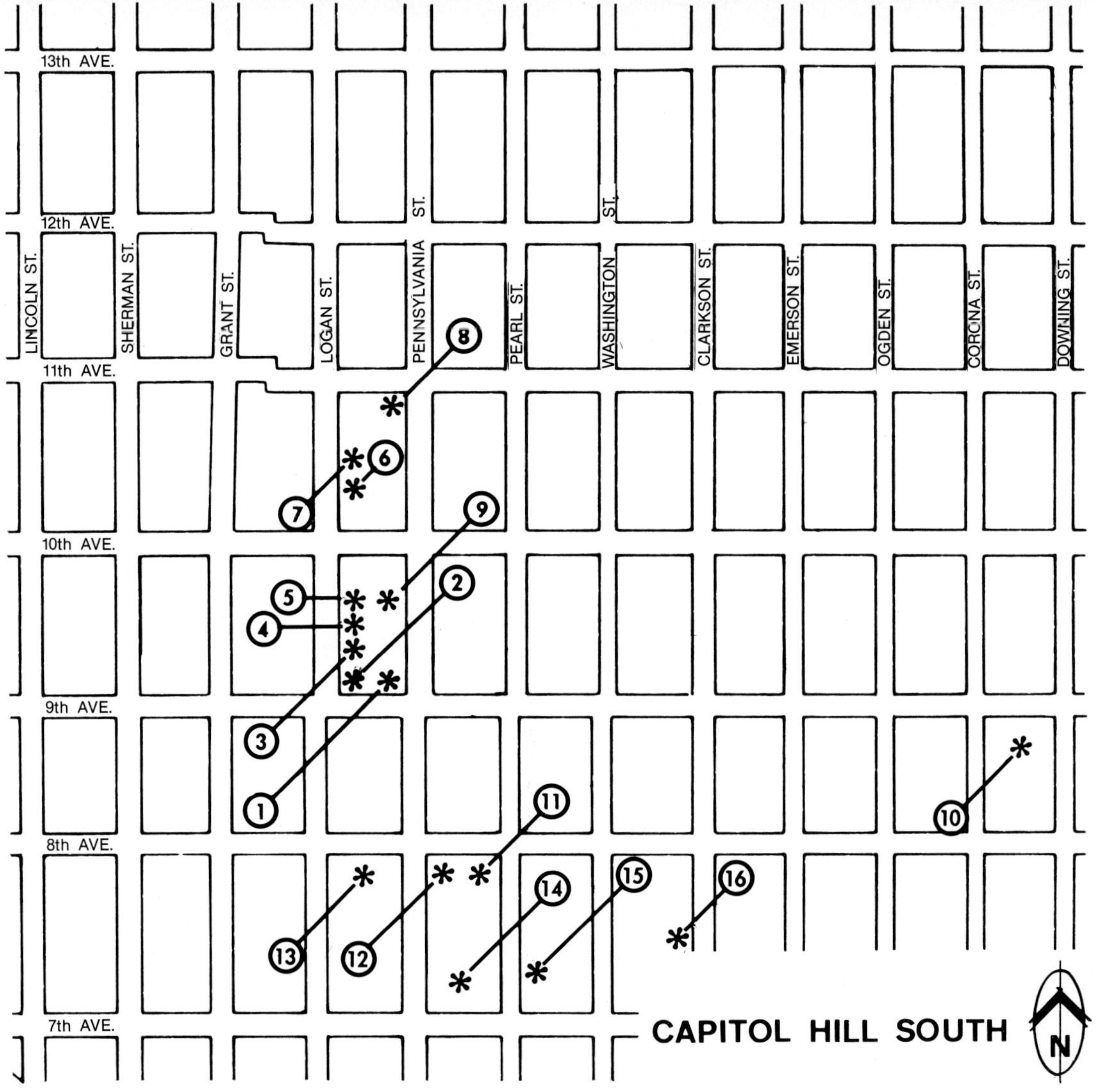
13th AVE.
12th AVE.
11th AVE.
10th AVE.
9th AVE.
8th AVE.
7th AVE.
LINCOLN ST.
SHERMAN ST.
GRANT ST.
LOGAN ST.
PENNSYLVANIA ST.
PEARL ST.
WASHINGTON ST.
CLARKSON ST.
EMERSON ST.
OGDEN ST.
CORONA ST.
DOWNING ST.
1
2
3
4
5
6
7
8
9
10
11
12
13
14
15
16
CAPITOL HILL SOUTH
N

J. Capitol Hill South

1. The Clemes-Lipe House

901 Pennsylvania Street

Constructed for C. L. Clemes in 1898, it was originally a Queen Anne style house (with large turrets on each end of the east facade) designed by Kidder and Wieger. Mrs. Clemes was the daughter of the well-known and wealthy mountain railroad engineer Edward Lipe. After the death of Mr. Clemes, Lipe's widow and her two sons moved into the house with Mrs. Clemes and in 1915 they extensively remodeled it, doubling its size and changing the overall design to the so-called "Newport" style.

Construction Date: *1898 and 1915*
Architect: *(Original) Kidder and Wieger*
(Addition) Not known
Style: *Newport*
Designation Number 57; February 9, 1974

2. The Hallett House

900 Logan Street

The first of four contiguous designated landmarks, this large house was built for Judge Moses Hallett, who had made a fortune in the silver and cattle businesses. Subsequently he served as the last territorial judge and the first federal judge in Colorado, as well as being the second dean of the University of Colorado Law School.

Although the house has forty-two rooms (and ten fireplaces), more space was added to it in 1900 by glassing-in the main porch.

Construction Date: *1892*
Architect: *Grable and Weber*
Style: *Queen Anne*
Designation Number 54; February 9, 1974

930

3. Residence
930 Logan Street

This is the first of four speculative houses built by broker-builder Fred A. Thompson, all designed by the same architect. It was sold in 1891 to John L. McNeil, president of the State National Bank.

Construction Date: *1890*
Architect: *Varian and Sterner*
Style: *Victorian Eclectic*
Designation Number 86; January 11, 1976

4. Residence

940 Logan Street

Very little is known of the early history of the second of Thompson's four speculative houses, but by 1945 it had been divided into fifteen apartments.

In the early 1970s it was purchased, completely renovated, and restored, and it now serves as luxury offices.

Construction Date: *1891*
Architect: *Varian and Sterner*
Style: *Georgian Revival*
Designation Number 55; February 9, 1974

5. **Residence**
950 Logan Street

The last of Thompson's speculative houses was sold in 1895 to wealthy retired Army officer Lafayette E. Campbell, who for many years had been involved in mining investment and ownership. Beautifully restored in recent years, it now serves as the headquarters office of prominent Denver realtor and well-known preservationist Mary Cornelia Rae.

Construction Date: *1893*
Architect: *Varian and Sterner*
Style: *Georgian Revival*
Designation Number 56; February 9, 1974

6. **Residence**
1030 Logan Street

Constructed for Joel W. Stearns, president of Mountain Electric Company, this house has recently been restored and converted to office use. It is one of the few remaining examples of the architectural work of Harry T. E. Wendell.

Construction Date: *1896*
Architect: *Harry T. E. Wendell*
Style: *Mission*
Designation Number 108; August 13, 1978

7. The Daly House

1034 Logan Street

For some years, this house was occupied by Thomas F. Daly, founder of the Capitol Life Insurance Company.

Construction Date: *1894*
Architect: *Not known*
Style: *Builder vernacular*
Designation Number 85; September 28, 1975

8. The Croke-Patterson-Campbell House

430 East Eleventh Avenue

One of the architectural gems of Capitol Hill, this house was constructed by Thomas E. Croke, a state senator credited with building Loretto Heights College and recognized as the nation's "Father of Irrigation." It was subsequently sold to Thomas H. Patterson, another state senator, who was a delegate to the Territorial Congress and a national leader of the Populist party. The house is a remarkable (and Denver's only surviving) example of the French Loire Valley Chateau style. Beautifully proportioned and extremely picturesque, its carriage house is also noteworthy.

Construction Date: *1890*
Architect: *Isaac Hodgson*
Style: *Chateauesque*
Designation Number 33; August 20, 1973
(listed on National Register)

9. The Taylor House

945 Pennsylvania Street

This house was built for Frank M. Taylor, an internationally known mining authority who worked extensively in the Rocky Mountain region. It is a most interesting, although by no means typical, example of its architectural style. The entrance hall, of an unusual octagonal shape with arched openings into seven spaces, is notable.

Construction Date: *1900*
Architect: *Not known*
Style: *Modified Mission*
Designation Number 58; February 9, 1974

MOORE SCHOOL

10. The Dora Moore School

846 Corona Street

Known for many years as the Corona School, it was renamed to honor Dora Moore, a longtime teacher and principal. Among its alumni are such prominent persons as Douglas Fairbanks, Paul Whiteman, Mamie Doud Eisenhower, and Judy Collins. The original structure, exhibiting some elements of the Romanesque style, is architecturally more significant than the east addition of some twenty years later.

Construction Date: *1889*
Architect: *Robert S. Roeschlaub*
Style: *Adaptive Romanesque Revival*
Designation Number 77; May 6, 1975
(listed on National Register)

11. The John Porter House

777 Pearl Street

This house was constructed for pioneer Denver entrepreneur and philanthropist John Porter. It is a rare (for Denver) and very pure example of the Jacobethan style.

Construction Date: *1923*
Architect: *Varian and Varian*
Style: *Jacobethan Revival*
Designation Number 75; May 6, 1975
(listed on National Register)

12. The Malo House

500 East Eighth Avenue

Constructed for Oscar L. Malo, who was the president of the Colorado Milling and Elevator Company, the house is a beautiful, serene structure embodying all the characteristics of its design style.

Construction Date: *1921*
Architect: *Harry C. Manning*
Style: *Spanish Colonial Revival*
Designation Number 74; April 6, 1975
(listed on National Register)

13. The Governor's Mansion

400 East Eighth Avenue

Built by Walter S. Cheesman (see Cheesman Memorial), founder of the Union Depot Company and the City Water Works, the house was later occupied by his daughter and her husband, John Evans II. It was sold in 1926 to Claude Boettcher. In 1960 the Boettcher family gave it to the state and it now serves as the Governor's Mansion.

It is known also as the Cheesman-Boettcher Mansion.

Construction Date: *1908*
Architect: *Marean and Norton*
Style: *Georgian and Neoclassical Revivals*
Designation Number 1; January 9, 1968
(listed on National Register)

14. The Grant-Humphreys Mansion
770 Pennsylvania Street

Built by James B. Grant, the third (and first Democrat) governor of Colorado as well as a founder of Colorado Women's College, it was purchased in 1917 by iron and oil magnate Albert E. Humphreys, a noted philanthropist. It was bequeathed to the state by his son, Ira B. Humphreys, in 1976, with the ground going to the city of Denver for use as a park. Now undergoing a complete restoration, it is used for offices, including those of Historic Denver, Inc.

Construction Date: *1902*
Architect: *Boal and Harnois*
Style: *Georgian and Neoclassical Revivals*
Designation Number 95; October 30, 1976
(listed on National Register)

15. The Foster-McCauley-Symes House
738 Pearl Street

Built for Alex C. Foster, prominent in Denver business circles, it was later owned by Vance McCauley and subsequently by U.S. District Court Judge J. Foster Symes.

Construction Date: *1905*
Architect: *Attributed to Frederick J. Sterner*
Style: *Georgian Revival*
Designation Number 34; August 20, 1973

16. The Adolph Zang House

709 Clarkson Street

This brick and sandstone house was built by Adolph Zang, a prominent early Denver businessman and the son of Philip Zang, who was the founder of the renowned Zang Brewery. The interior woodwork is unusually diverse and finely executed. The house boasts an unusual—and original—burglar alarm system.

Its carriage house on the north side has a pleasing, picturesque quality.

Construction Date: *1902*
Architect: *F. C. Eberly*
Style: *Neoclassical Revival*
Designation Number 99; June 12, 1977
(listed on National Register)

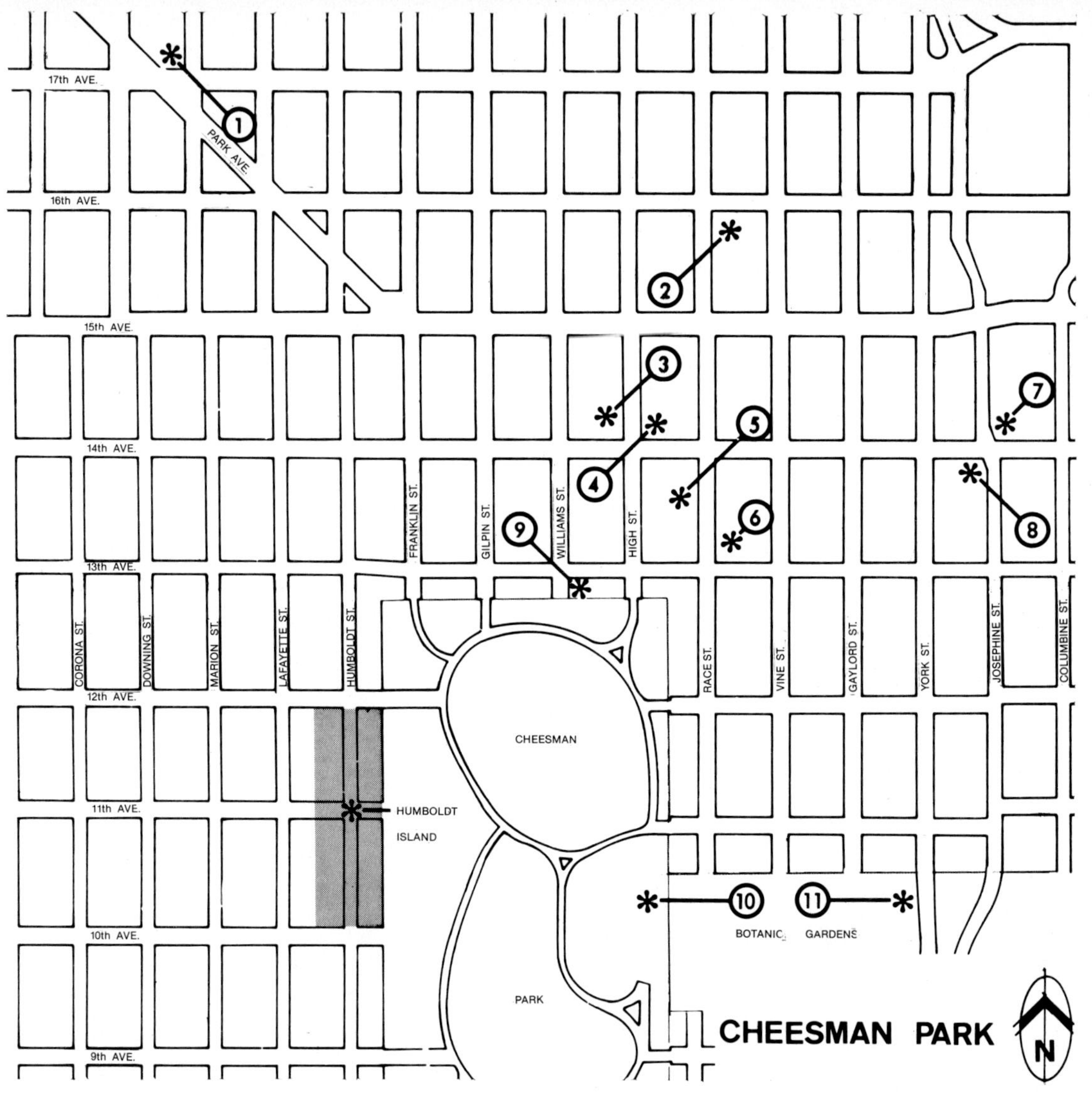
17th AVE.
PARK AVE.
16th AVE.
15th AVE.
14th AVE.
13th AVE.
12th AVE.
11th AVE.
10th AVE.
9th AVE.
CORONA ST.
DOWNING ST.
MARION ST.
LAFAYETTE ST.
HUMBOLDT ST.
FRANKLIN ST.
GILPIN ST.
WILLIAMS ST.
HIGH ST.
RACE ST.
VINE ST.
GAYLORD ST.
YORK ST.
JOSEPHINE ST.
COLUMBINE ST.
CHEESMAN
PARK
HUMBOLDT
ISLAND
BOTANIC GARDENS
1
2
3
4
5
6
7
8
9
10
11
N
CHEESMAN PARK

K. Cheesman Park Area

1. Residence

1129 East Seventeenth Avenue

This spacious house, prominently situated on the diagonal of Park Avenue at Seventeenth Avenue, was built for Leopold Rosenzweig in the early 1880s. Recently converted to offices by and for the use of the publisher of this book, it is an outstanding example of preservation by adaptive reuse. The strength of its design and architectural features are much enhanced by the sensitive exterior renovation.

Construction Date: *Early 1880s*
Architect: *Not known*
Style: *Modified Italianate*
Designation Number 106; November 13, 1977

2. The Raymond House

1572 Race Street

This gray sandstone house was built for Wilbur S. Raymond, a Denver investment banker. Much enhanced by its recent exterior restoration, it has a number of notable features, especially the large stained-glass window on the north side and the palladian window on the south. The unusual window next to the entrance porch demonstrates a new principle: an arch apparently supported by a post centered on a horizontal lintel!

(See also: 1200 Pennsylvania Street.)

Construction Date: *1889*
Architect: *William Lang*
Style: *Richardsonian Romanesque*
Designation Number 70; November 16, 1974
(listed on National Register)

3. Residence
1437 High Street

The residence of a number of prominent Denver families, the house eventually deteriorated to the point of condemnation by the city. It was rescued by complete restoration and now is utilized for offices.

Construction Date: *1894*
Architect: *Attributed to Frederick J. Sterner*
Style: *Victorian Eclectic*
Designation Number 93; July 18, 1976

4. The Sykes-Nicholson House
1410 High Street

This house was built for the Reverend Richard E. Sykes and sold in 1899 to Mrs. Eugenie Kountze Nicholson, whose husband was the author of the mystery novel House of a Thousand Candles. *The house has recently undergone a notable restoration and conversion for office use.*

Construction Date: *1897*
Architect: *Attributed to Frederick J. Sterner*
Style: *Georgian Revival*
Designation Number 92; July 18, 1976

5. The Adams-Fitzell House

1359 Race Street

One of a number of speculative houses constructed in this block by real estate developer Ernest F. Thomas, it was first occupied by Lafayette E. Campbell (see 950 Logan Street) and purchased in 1892 by cattle baron George Henry Adams. Since 1919 it has been occupied by the Grant R. Fitzell family, who have carefully maintained this pure example of the Shingle style.

Construction Date: *1890*
Architect: *Kidder and Humphreys*
Style: *Shingle*
Designation Number 76; May 6, 1975

6. **The Pope-Thompson-Wasson House**
1320 Race Street

Constructed in 1894, the house is one of the few remaining Denver examples of the work of noted architect Harry T. E. Wendell. The dynamic interplay of arches on the west and south facades is especially delightful.

(See also: Ivy Chapel.)

Construction Date: *1894*
Architect: *Harry T. E. Wendell*
Style: *Victorian Eclectic*
Designation Number 23; April 29, 1972

7. The Bosworth House

1400 Josephine Street

Constructed for Mrs. Daniel Skinner, it was purchased in 1904 by Mrs. Leona Bosworth, the widow of Joab Bosworth, who founded the Denver Fire Clay Company. The Bosworth family members were important early Denver business and civic leaders.

Construction Date: *1899*
Architect: *Not known*
Style: *Shingle*
Designation Number 73; January 27, 1975

8. Residence
1375 Josephine Street

This house was built in 1892 for Russell Gates, founder of the Russell Gates Mercantile Company. It is Denver's almost classic example of a house in the style of Henry Hobson Richardson, generally recognized as one of the three greatest American-born architects (in company with Louis Sullivan and Frank Lloyd Wright). The design is a well-defined shingle style with a rusticated stone ground floor. The Romanesque arches, however, are not typical of the style.

Construction Date: *1892*
Architect: *H. Chatten*
Style: *Shingle and Richardsonian Romanesque*
Designation Number 104; October 9, 1977

1200

9. The Tears-McFarlane House

1200 Williams Street

This house was built for the associate counsel of the New York Central Railroad, Daniel W. Tears. It was sold in 1937 to Frederick McFarlane. It is a good example of the Neocolonial Georgian architectural style.

Construction Date: *1898*
Architect: *Frederick J. Sterner*
Style: *Georgian Revival*
Designation Number 29; January 22, 1973
(listed on National Register)

10. The Cheesman Memorial
Cheesman Park

This serene pavilion, constructed of Colorado yule marble, was presented to the city of Denver in memory of Walter S. Cheesman (see Governor's Mansion) by his widow, Alice Foster Cheesman, and his daughter, Gladys Cheesman Evans. Beautifully sited on the east side of the park, it commands a spectacular western view.

Construction Date: *1907*
Architect: *Marean and Norton*
Style: *Neoclassical Revival*
Designation Number 45; November 26, 1973

11. The Boettcher Conservatory
1005 York Street

This striking structure was erected in Denver's Botanic Gardens as a memorial to Mr. and Mrs. Claude Boettcher (see Governor's Mansion). Constructed on the principle of an inverted catenary curve, its reinforced concrete ribs soar skyward with breathtaking grace and delicacy.

Construction Date: *1964*
Architects: *Victor Hornbein and Edward D. White, Jr.*
Style: *Modern*
Designation Number 46; November 26, 1973

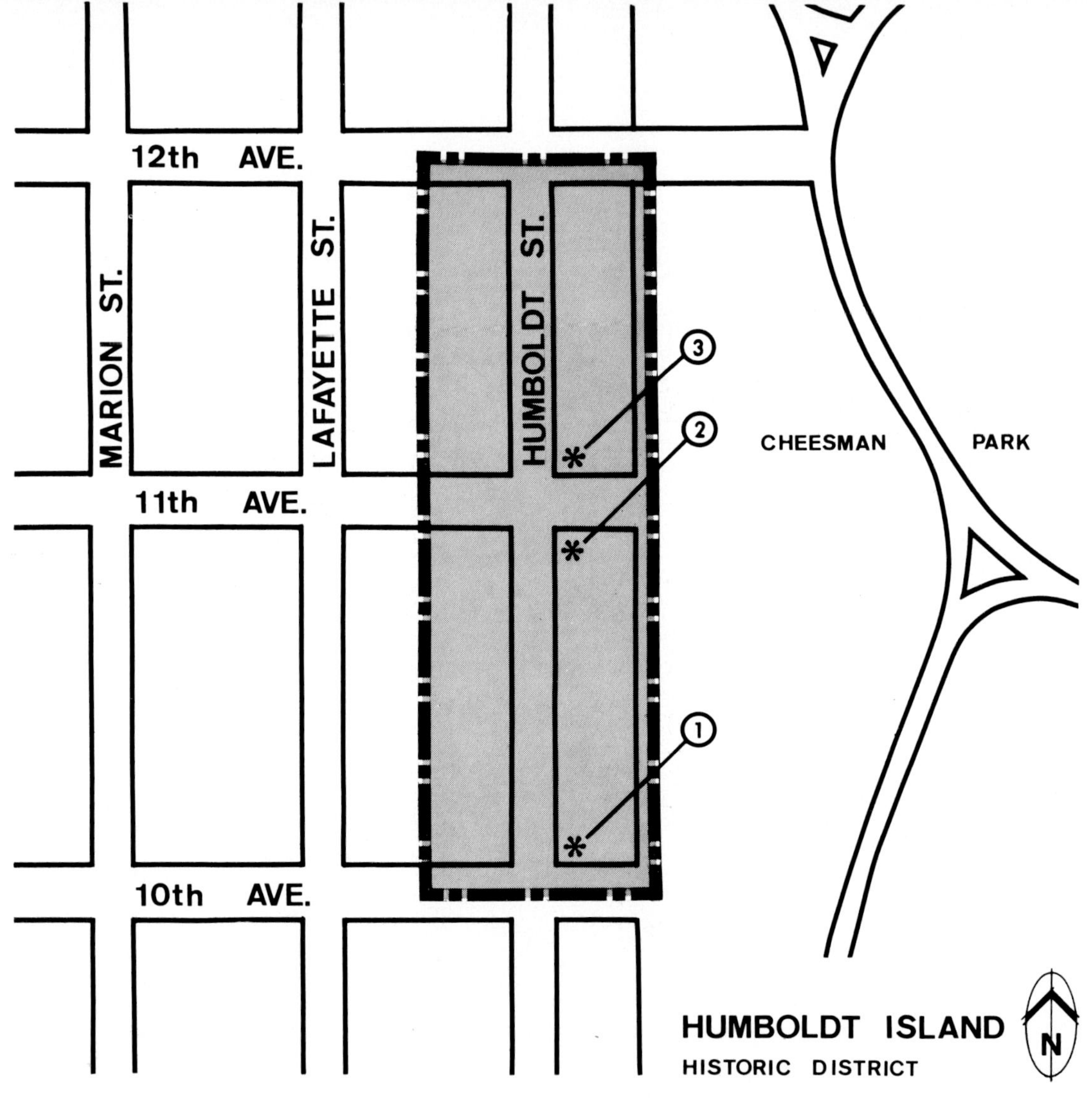
12th AVE.
11th AVE.
10th AVE.
MARION ST.
LAFAYETTE ST.
HUMBOLDT ST.
CHEESMAN PARK
3
2
1
N
HUMBOLDT ISLAND
HISTORIC DISTRICT

L. The Humboldt Island Historic District

The twenty-four houses comprising this district, all constructed between 1895 and 1920, display a wide range of residential styles. Built in that unfortunate period when architects were timidly seeking new forms, few of them display the vigor and design sense of the preceding High Victorian era. They are, however, large well-maintained houses and accurately reflect the architectural taste of the period in which they were built, and for this reason they are important. The best examples, in an architectural sense, are shown on the following pages.

Designation Number: District 2; April 29, 1972
(listed on National Register)

1. **The Stoiber-Reed-Humphreys House**
1022 Humboldt Street

Designed by the well-known architectural firm of Marean and Norton, this house was constructed in 1907 for the widow of mining engineer Edward G. Stoiber. A fine example of the imposing Second Renaissance Revival style, it has a grand two-story-high glass-covered atrium and a swimming pool in the basement!

Humboldt Island Historic District

NOT A
THROUGH
STREET
NO
PARKING

2. The Thompson-Henry House
1070 Humbolt Street

This house was built in 1905 for Alonzo H. Thompson, a prominent Denver realtor who lived there for twelve years. Designed by the popular architectural firm of the Baerresen Brothers (Danish-born and European-trained) in the Georgian Revival style, it is noted for its exceptionally fine interiors.

Humboldt Island Historic District

3. The Brown-Mackenzie-McDougal House
1100 Humboldt Street

Occupied for the last thirty-eight years by prominent Denver attorney Robert L. McDougal, this house was built in 1903 to the design of architect Eugene R. Rice. Vigorous and delightful, it is a wonderful example of the Late Eclectic style, boasting an unusual oriel, Gothic windows throughout the second floor, and a charming second floor balcony on the south side. The entrance canopy is a later addition.

Humboldt Island Historic District

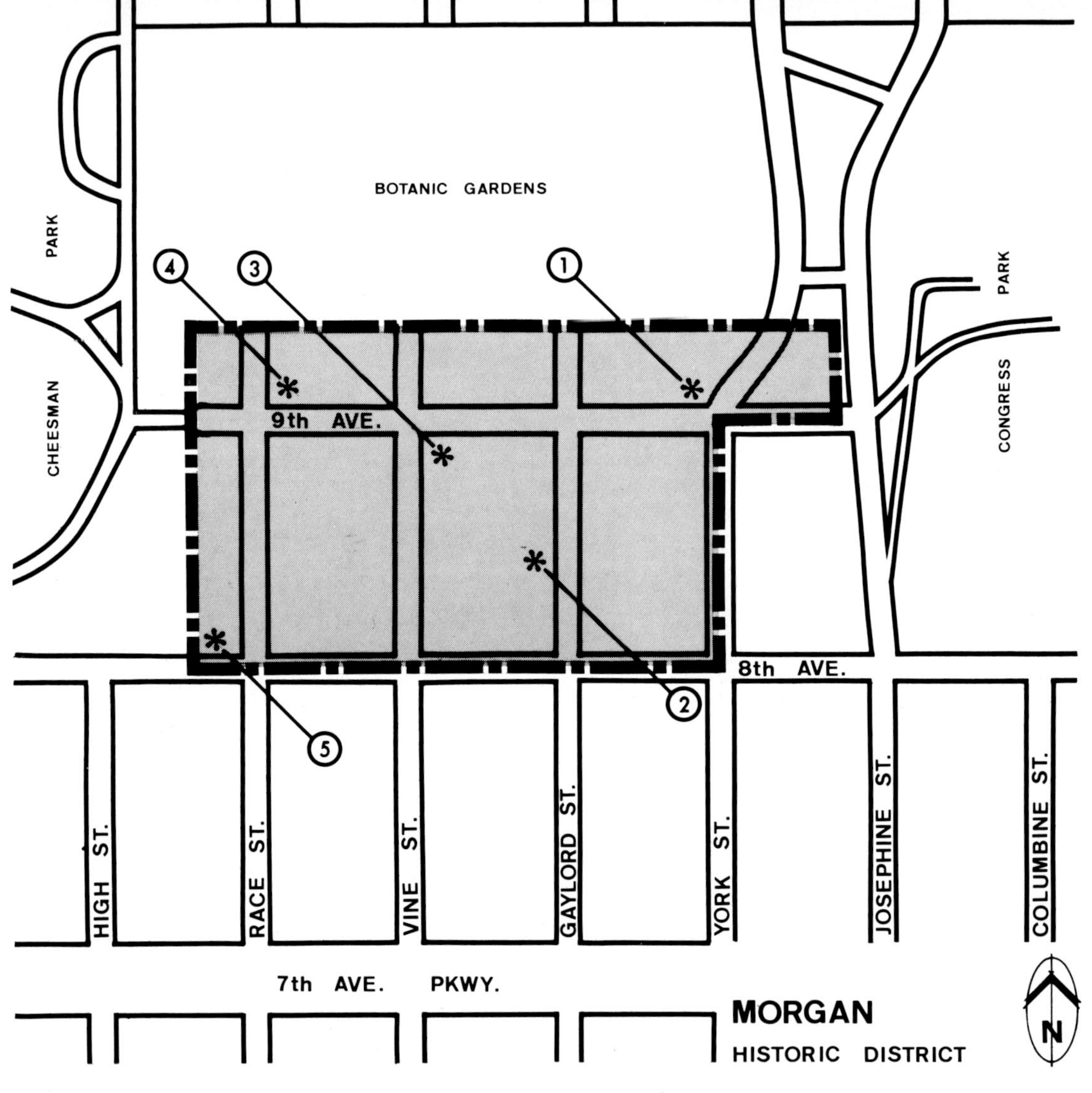
BOTANIC GARDENS
CHEESMAN
PARK
CONGRESS
PARK
9th AVE.
8th AVE.
7th AVE. PKWY.
HIGH ST.
RACE ST.
VINE ST.
GAYLORD ST.
YORK ST.
JOSEPHINE ST.
COLUMBINE ST.
1
2
3
4
5
N
MORGAN
HISTORIC DISTRICT

M. The Morgan Historic District

Composed of forty-five houses, of which thirty-eight were constructed in the twenty-year period between 1910 and 1930, this district is a showcase of residential architectural styles. Named for the original subdivider, Samuel B. Morgan, it is an interesting architectural contrast to the slightly earlier Humboldt Island District, just across the park. The works of no less than twelve prominent architects are represented here, some as many as five times. The list of original owners reads like a Who's Who of Denver *and includes among others Henry Porter, William Day Downs, James J. Waring, O. W. Toll, Mason A. Lewis, Stephen Knight, William E. Porter, Richard Crawford Campbell, Roger D. Knight, William Lloyd Petrikin, Daniel Millett, J. Quigg Newton, and Stephen Knight, Jr.*

Designation Number: District 8; February 23, 1978

BOTANIC GARDENS HOUSE

1. The Botanic Gardens House
909 York Street

Constructed for Richard Crawford Campbell, it was purchased by Ruth Porter Waring in the 1960s and given to the Botanic Gardens. Like so many of the works of architect J. J. B. Benedict, it is difficult to classify stylistically. Eclectic—yes, but this house does display many elements of the Jacobethan style.

Construction Date: *1926*
Architect: *J. J. B. Benedict*
Style: *Benedict*
Designation Number 47; November 26, 1973

2. The Mason A. Lewis House
845 Gaylord Street

Designed by architect Lester Varian and constructed in 1922 for Mason A. Lewis, this house is a fine example of the then very popular Spanish Colonial Revival style.

Morgan Historic District

3. The Daniel Millett House

860 Vine Street

This serene and elegant example of the Georgian Revival style (predominantly Federal Period) was built in 1920 for transplanted New England businessman Daniel Millett. Over the protests of the architects, William E. and Arthur A. Fisher, Mrs. Millet insisted that the large entrance hall be extended entirely through the house—with very successful results. The carved cornucopia over the front door is a notable exterior feature.

Morgan Historic District

4. The Mrs. Tyson Dines House
900 Race Street

This meticulously detailed Georgian Revival house, in the Neo-Adamesque mode, was built in 1931 for the widow of prominent Denver attorney and civic leader Tyson Dines. The historical correctness of the exterior details (a characteristic for which its architect, Harry Manning, was noted) makes the house an interesting, although not outstanding, example of the style. The very refined interior detailing, in the Adam style, displays a notable delicacy and lightness.

Morgan Historic District

5. The Sullivan House
801 Race Street

The rather abstract composition of the main (east) facade of this 1928 house hardly prepares one for the explosiveness of its elaborately colonnaded west facade. Designed by architect J. J. B. Benedict, in its strictest sense this is a classic example of the "town house."

Morgan Historic District

Addendum

No such document would be complete without a word about the Denver Landmark Preservation Commission, why it exists, and what it does.

The commission was created in 1967 by council ordinance, which states in part that "... the protection, enhancement, perpetuation and use of structures and districts of historical, architectural, or geographic significance ... is a public necessity and is required in the interest of prosperity, civic pride, and the general welfare of the people." Under this ordinance the commission has three basic responsibilities: identification of structures or districts that have unique historic, architectural, or geographic significance; nomination of those structures or districts for landmark designation; and administration of the ordinance provisions pertaining to the exterior renovation or demolition of designated structures.

The commission is composed of nine members, all appointed by the mayor on the basis of nominations submitted by the Denver Planning Board (three), the State Historical Society (two), the American Institute of Architects (two), and two appointments without limitations.

The original members of the commission and their terms of office follow:

Helen M. Arndt	*1967–Present*
Frances Fuller	*1967–Present*
Philip Milstein	*1967–Present*
Alan Fisher	*1967–1978*
Gerald T. Hart	*1967–1974*

Robert L. Stearns	*1967–1972*
James Sudler	*1967–1972*
Philip Atchison	*1967–1969*

Subsequent commission appointments:

Edward D. White, Jr.	*1969–Present*
Thomas Hornsby Ferril	*1972–Present*
Langdon E. Morris, Jr.	*1973–Present*
Joseph B. Barry	*1974–Present*
James C. Morgan	*1978–Present*
Barbara J. Norgren	*1979–Present*

The commission relies on the Denver Planning Office for its staff support, including the commission secretary and such technical and clerical help as may be required. Since 1974 the commission has been fortunate to have as secretary the able and personable David A. Wicks, whose untiring efforts have done so much to facilitate its operation.

The question is often raised about Denver structures that are listed on the National Register of Historic Places and yet do not have Denver landmark designation. This situation could result from either of two things: the structure does not meet Landmark Commission criteria (which are more stringent than those of the National Register); or the building owner requested that the commission not nominate his building, a request the commission has always honored. Because of owner objections, many of Denver's greatest landmarks remain without designation. The four buildings on the following pages are representative examples of these obvious, yet undesignated, Denver landmarks.

Brown
Hotel

The Brown Palace Hotel
Seventeenth Street and Broadway

The finest extant example of architect Frank E. Edbrooke's work, both interior and exterior, the Brown Palace has been a downtown landmark since 1890.

(Listed on National Register)

UNION STATION
TRAVEL TRAIN
UNION STATION
1914
NO RIGHT TURN
STOP

Union Station
Seventeenth and Wynkoop streets

Denver's only example of the Beaux Arts Classicism style, it provides a strong visual terminus to Seventeenth Street.

(Listed on National Register)

NO DOUBLE TURN
ONLY
CHAMPA
ONLY
WORLD SAVINGS
WORLD SAVINGS

The Boston Building
Seventeenth and Champa streets

Widely acknowledged to be Denver's finest surviving nineteenth century office building, it was designed in the Richardsonian Romanesque style by Boston architects Andrews, Jacques, and Rantoul.

(Listed on National Register)

Central Presbyterian Church
East Seventeenth Avenue and Sherman Street

Designed in the Richardsonian Romanesque style, this 1890 church is one of Frank E. Edbrooke's great masterpieces.

(Listed on National Register)

Building/Map Index

Note: The first number refers to the page on which a building is discussed or a geographical section is introduced. The letter-number combination refers to the map on which a building appears and to its numerical designation on the map.

Index of Architects